The Uncommon
Book of Prayer

The Uncommon Book of Prayer

Recovering the Spiritual Discipline of Prayer

Dr. Larry Wayne Ellis

iUniverse, Inc.
New York   Bloomington

iUniverse books may be ordered through booksellers or by contacting:

iUniverse
1663 Liberty Drive
Bloomington, IN 47403
www.iuniverse.com
1-800-Authors (1-800-288-4677)

ISBN: 978-1-4401-2386-3 (sc)
ISBN: 978-1-4401-2521-8 (dj)
ISBN: 978-1-4401-2387-0 (ebook)

Printed in the United States of America

iUniverse rev. date: 03/18/2009

Dedicated to my siblings,

Margaret

Ervin (deceased)

Mary

Wanda

Alden Patrick

Philbert (deceased)

Kathy

Contents

Acknowledgments

I want to thank Ms. Nola Butler for her editing expertise. She is largely responsible for the book coming to fruition. The P.A.C.T. ministry, of which Mrs. Eileen White gives outstanding leadership, has supported my ministry beyond my wildest dreams. Finally, I want to thank the Pilgrim Baptist Church of San Mateo that is an authentic Acts 2:42 fellowship.

Preface

I read a statement in an article—the origin of which I do not recall—that said, "Little things done well go unnoticed; but left undone, they make a huge difference." If there is a grain of truth in this adage (and I think there is), what is the impact if great things are left undone?

I am both challenged and convicted by the promise and potential of 2 Chronicles 7:14: "If my people, who are called by my name, shall humble themselves, and *pray*, and seek my face, and turn from their *wicked* ways; then will I hear from heaven, and will forgive their sin, and will heal their land" (emphasis added). God invites His people to pray, and He promises healing and forgiveness in response to those prayers.

Our planet is in grave peril. Nations are bent on self-destruction or determined to destroy other nations. Economies are failing and disease is rampant. Where are the people of God? What are we doing about these problems, or about the plights of people who are trapped in despair? Where are the prayers? Is it possible that God's people are failing to make any difference because we are failing in the ministry of prayer?

The title of this work is based on my belief that the ministry of prayer is no longer common among God's people. The chapters were lectures on prayer that I shared during midweek worship services in our church. The motivation for writing this book developed from the three-month sabbatical that I took at the end of 2007. During my times of prayer, the Holy Spirit convinced me that the lack of power in our church was attributable to a lack of prayer. When I shared this with other spiritual leaders across our country, they agreed with my findings.

I am presenting this work to the larger Christian community because this teaching impacted our band of believers at Pilgrim Church in San Mateo, California. It is my prayer that the insights offered here will inspire the reader to pray.

Introduction

Our Lord Jesus Christ is the greatest gift that God gave to humanity. According to Christian theology, Jesus was both human and divine, without mixture. In His own words, He was from the Father and did only His Father's will. In John 5:30, Jesus says, "I can of mine own self do nothing: as I hear, I judge: and my judgment is just; because I seek not mine own will, but the will of the Father which hath sent me" (KJV).

Jesus is so much more than our language can capture. One fact that cannot be refuted is that the Lord was a person of prayer. His disciples were so moved by the power that resulted from His talks with the Father that they asked, "Lord, teach us to pray."

Our Lord was a premier preacher, healer, mentor, and so much more. However, His disciples' request to learn to pray is recorded in Scripture!

Many modern believers are asking for wealth, health, and supernatural anointing. Few are asking to learn the discipline of prayer.

Prayer is uncommon in our fellowships. The subject of prayer is preached, but the practice of prayer is neglected. Our churches are increasing in numbers but not in the personal growth that can only come from spending time in the presence of the Lord.

Jesus prayed before calling the Twelve. He prayed before performing the miracles of healing and before the miracle of raising Lazarus.

Why has prayer fallen into such disuse and abuse? One possible answer is that we have learned to do so much without God. Our advances in so many areas have given both sinners and saints a sense of independence, if not arrogant self-sufficiency.

In this work, I will discuss prayer that works, prayer according to Jesus, keys to answered prayer, our Lord's Prayer, and finally, a model for praying.

Prayer is the key to unlocking power in the pew as well as in the pulpit.

Prayer anchored the work of our Lord on earth. In Luke 18:1, Jesus says that men ought always to pray, and not to faint (KJV).

Jesus engaged in prayer before, during, and after the cross event.

John Wesley, the founder of the Methodist movement, was so convinced of God's personal investment in prayer that he taught that God does nothing except in answer to prayer!

Yet today, prayer often is dismissed as unnecessary or ineffective.

It is my prayer that this book on prayer will inspire the reader to pray more often and with greater confidence.

1

Prayer That Works

Matthew 21:21–22
John 15:7

Here is what Jesus said about prayer in Matthew 21:21–22:

> So Jesus answered and said to them, "Assuredly, I say to you, if you have faith and do not doubt, you will not only do what was done to the fig tree, but also if you say to this mountain, 'Be removed and be cast into the sea,' it will be done. And whatever things you ask in prayer, believing, you will receive." (NKJV)

Now, do not rush over this Scripture; let that soak in. Jesus said, "*Whatever* thing you ask in prayer." That means anything that you ask for in prayer—not doubting, but believing that whatever you ask for, you will receive—you *shall* receive it. Not some things, but *anything* that you ask for in prayer.

Keep that thought in mind as you turn to John 15:7. Watch this!

> "If you abide in me ... that is to dwell in, spend time with, get to know in an intimate way ... if you live in Me and I live in you, My words abide or live in you. You will ask whatsoever you desire and it shall be done."

Now, put those two thoughts together. If you do not doubt what you believe, whatever you ask for, you will receive. That's what Matthew, one of Jesus' disciples, wrote. Another disciple, John, wrote that if you abide in Him and His words abide in you, then you can ask anything and you will receive it.

Let's be honest: how many people do you know who say they are believers, but walk around every day with their needs and desires pretty much unmet? How many of us, if we were honest, would have to say that we do not have much of what we really want? If the Lord Jesus said, "If you abide in Me, you can ask for whatever you want and you'll get it," and He also said, "If My words are in you, whatever you desire, you can have," then why are most of us walking around with our needs unmet? More importantly, why is it that with this promissory note given to us, many of us, as believers, do not spend any time praying? We cannot get anything if we do not ask for anything. So, if we do not ask, but He has promised that He is going to give us whatever we ask for, then, as one of my church members would say, "What the problem is?" Why is it that the Lord gives us this undefined promissory note and yet, if we are honest about it, most of us walk around or live our lives with our needs unmet? *What the problem is?* Let's look at it!

John Knox

"God calls ordinary people and gives them a passion and a purpose. It is their job to pray it into reality."

John Knox, considered the father of the Presbyterian denomination, was a tremendous man of prayer. Listen to what this man of God said: "Prayer can shape reality." Passages from Matthew 21 and John 15:7 shaped Knox's thinking. In other words, whatever you desire your reality to be, you can shape that reality through prayer. That's how powerful prayer is! You can actually shape your own reality through your prayer life. I want you to get what he is saying—that your reality does not have to be handed to you by somebody else. God has given you the power to shape your own reality.

Form

Let's be honest. Many of us do not hold that concept of prayer. I share with you that I did not hold that concept either. Why? Because you and I learned prayer as a matter of *form*, not *shape*.

Here's what happened. Prayer was given to us. We were taught by our forefathers that we had to pray at certain times, and that our prayers had to be of a certain length. That length had to do with how we were able to go around the world—sending God to the hospital, the prison, the convalescent home, the war-torn countries, and all of that. We were taught from our forefathers that the Bible says something like, "Our walls were not the four walls of our casket, and our bed was not our cooling board, and our sheets were not winding sheets." That is the way our forefathers prayed.

Our forefathers also thought that prayer had to do with the number of words that were prayed. You could not pray like Nehemiah and just say, "Lord, remember me." You could not pray like Paul and say, "Lord, stand by me." We were taught that our prayers had to be made up of many words. That's how we got the "flowery" language of prayer: "Lord, as I stand here in the evening by and by, trying to turn to Thee with some sincere thanks, I want to thank You that You allowed my golden moments to roll on, that You lengthened the brickly threads of my unprofitable life and allowed my golden moments to roll on ..."

This prayer style was handed down as a means of contacting God when, honestly, what it did was become a *form* that kept us from really conversing with God.

After the lengthy time and the flowery language, next came the tune—"My Lord" (sung), and all of that. You had to tune it up. You had to sound it out. Then, as you did that, the congregation would get with you. "Pray, Deacon!" "Pray, Rabbi!" "Pray, Mother!"

After the prayer, someone would always come up to you and say, "Ms. Clara, thank you for that prayer!" What was really happening— without us realizing it—was that the prayer was really toward us, not toward God. That became our *form*.

Most of us who learned how to pray did so in that style. We never checked to see whether or not our prayers were answered. We said our prayers, and we had our prayer meetings and prayer times. But it did not work for our forefathers, and it does not work for us.

Consequently, people stopped praying because they couldn't pray like our forefathers prayed or like "Ms. Clara" prayed. Their response was, "I can't pray like that." Most people will not pray in public now because they desire to pray like someone else. So they do not pray. The whole idea of prayer is not to be heard by men and women but to be heard by God. And God is the only One whom you and I have to please. Bruce Wilkerson shares his journey of coming to faith in prayer.

"In the Prayer of Jabez you can expect God's astounding answers to prayer as a regular part of your life's experience. Once the believer is convinced that God does answer prayer then he or she will pray with confidence and regularity." [1]

In Matthew 6:5–8, Jesus said that we are not to stand on the street corners and in marketplaces to pray to be seen of man, for then we have our reward. He said this of the Pharisees: "They pray with many flowery words so they can impress man, but they have their reward" (paraphrased). We have been really influenced by *form*. The result has been that most of us are not excited about praying. We do not understand the possibilities because we do not understand what prayer can really do.

If you and I ever discovered that prayer is really the force that moves the hand of God, then that is what we would spend most of our time doing. John Wesley, the father of the Methodist denomination, said it like this: "God does nothing except in answer to prayer." The Lord said it like this: "You have not because you asked not" (James 4:2). If this powerful medium, one that can move the God of the universe, is at our disposal, then why do we not give ourselves over to it? *What is the problem?*

It may be that we have not caught the vision of Jesus.

The Lord did not do anything until *after* He prayed. Let us think about that. In preparation for calling the Twelve, Jesus spent the whole night in prayer. Wait a minute, now. He is God, right? He knows everything. Yet, when Jesus was preparing to do anything of great significance, He spent the whole night in prayer. If Jesus is God and Jesus knows everything, then why does Jesus do that? Why not just thirty minutes? Why not just an hour? Why did Jesus spend whole entire nights in prayer? He did so because the Lord gives Himself to that which is most valuable. Prayer becomes not just a means of getting something from God but a means of spending time in the very presence of God.

In other words, the more you pray, the more you enjoy just being in the Lord's presence. As you do this, you find that you don't get in God's presence just to ask Him for stuff but because you sincerely want to be with Him. Just with Him! And you're glad to be with Him. Then fifteen minutes becomes thirty minutes; thirty minutes becomes an hour; an hour becomes two hours ... because you love being in His presence. Before you realize it, television becomes less of a draw—not because you don't like television but because you would simply rather be in God's presence.

Prayer becomes an obsession. Luke 18:1 says, "Men are ought always to pray" (KJV). Why?

1. Because there is nothing better to do?

2. To get something from God?

3. Because if you pray, you will understand the very will of God and the very heart of God. Then you start asking for what you know the Father wants to give you. You pray because you know that God is going to meet your needs anyway, so you desire to spend time with Him.

What if the only time my sons ever contacted me was when they needed something? As a human being, I would get tired of that. I would say to them, "You never call just to come by and hang with Dad. What do you want?" "Well, you know, you know ..." If every time they stopped by they just wanted something, that would upset me. I would conclude that they really didn't love me and that they were just using me. I would say to them, "If I ever get to the point where I cannot give you what you are asking for, you have already shown me that you are not going to come around anymore. If I don't have anything to give you, then you have little desire to be in my presence."

Now, if that is true in the human arena, how much more is it true in the divine arena? Is it that God is saying, "You do not talk to Me because you do not really love Me? And the only time you want to talk is when you get into a crisis, something is going on, somebody is sick, and/or somebody is out of work. Then you run to Me. As soon as the problem is solved or the crisis ends, then you have nothing to say to Me." Maybe God is saying to us, "I know why you do not pray. It is because you do not really want to spend time with Me ... just for Me. You do not love Me well enough to give Me some time."

John Knox said it like this: "All God wants is to invite ordinary people into a relationship with Him." In other words, God is not asking that you be a super saint. God is not asking that you possess some unusual talents or abilities in order to enter into an intimate relationship with Him. As John Knox said, all God wants is ordinary people. How many of us are ordinary? I know I am. God wants ordinary people to discover their passion. Ordinary people who understand their passion will receive power from God. That power is contracted through prayer. God wants to use you, an ordinary person, and give you a passion for something. He then gives you the power to carry out that passion. And you can actualize all of that through prayer.

Prayer becomes the way in which we get in touch with God. In John 13:14, Jesus said "If you ask anything in My name, that will I do it." Now, we have got to work with this. To paraphrase Psalm 37:4, delight yourselves in the Lord, and He will give you the desires of your hearts.

Did I leave anything out? Remember:

John Knox says that God wants just ordinary men and women, gives them each a passion, and then gives them power that is actualized through prayer.

The psalmist says, "What God wants us to do is to delight ourselves in Him, and then He will give us the desires of our hearts."

Now, watch as we put it together:

In the books of Matthew and John, Jesus says that if you ask anything, He will do it. Carte blanche!

Then the psalmist says—let me paraphrase a little: Delight yourself in the Lord, and He will give it to you.

So this all goes together now. What is the Bible saying? That if we spend enough time in prayer, then the very thought pattern of God becomes ours.

Philippians 2:5 says, "Let this mind be in you, which was also in Christ Jesus" (KJV). Jesus is going to give you the very mind of Christ in prayer. Then you are going to begin to think like God thinks and love like God loves, which, in turn, formulates what you ask for.

Shape

Now everything that you ask for, you start to receive. You now have the mind of Christ. You have the heart of God. Now we can ask God for certain things. That is called *intercession*.

God wants to save people through Jesus Christ. God wants to heal the sick. God wants to encourage the sad. God wants to bless those who need a blessing. God wants you to be an instrument of peace. So you start spending all your time doing that. Give yourself over to that. When someone has a need, ask to pray with him or her, but no asking for a Cadillac, a Mercedes, a house, a husband, a promotion—none of that.

For instance, if I know of a need that my son has, I might ask him, "Can I pray with you?" We pray together, and then later, with that prayer in mind, he tells me that God has answered his prayer. He is very happy. This is an example of my son delighting himself in God, and he finds out that, "Oh, man, that works!" So now the only thing he wants to receive is what God wants.

Perhaps I ask my wife what her need is. She says, "My only niece does not know the Lord." Well, let's pray. And we continue to pray until her niece comes to know God.

These are examples of how we begin to give ourselves over to what God sees as important: delighting ourselves in Him, praying, fasting, and sharing.

Let me tell you what God does. Everything has to do with God's will. In Matthew 6:25–33, Jesus says that the Heavenly Father knows that you need food, clothing, shelter, and good health. But, He says, seek first the kingdom of God. Delight yourself first in the kingdom of God and His righteousness, and then watch what God will do!

Let me share how we have it in the wrong order. "God, give me a husband, give me a wife, give me a job, give me a car, heal my body, make my enemies leave me alone, and, if You do all of that, God, I promise You I will leave You. I promise You I will become spiritually cold. I promise You I will never put You first anymore. I will always have something more important to do when You ask me to do something."

I have my desires inverted. You see, if I can get enough stuff or enough money, then I do not have to ask God for it. If I can be healthy enough so that I don't have to worry about dying, then I can insulate myself from ever really needing God because I have everything that I need. What I will do is pay God lip service, but I will not give myself to Him because, really, I do not need Him (Isa. 29:13, Matt. 15:8).

Most of us spend our time trying to get our lives in order such that we do not need God. Then we spend the rest of our lives pretending that we love Him when, in reality, we have given ourselves over to things that are not at all God-worthy or God-conscious.

I am fifty-seven years old, and I know it is late in life for me. But I do not want to be like Tom Brady. I do not want to be like Denzel Washington. I do not want to be like Donald Trump. I do not want to be like Tom Cruise.

I want to be like Jesus. That is my desire. I do not want to impress anybody but Jesus. I do not want to do what anybody but the Lord tells me to do. I want to give Him my time; I want Him to be first in my life. I have come to the conclusion that I want Jesus to be my all in all. That is all I want. I do not want a bigger car. I do not want a bigger house. I do not want more money. I do not want any of that. I just want to be like Jesus. And I find myself spending more and more and more time with Him.

My wife and I had no church home for three months. We couldn't say to anyone, "Our church is located here," or, "Our church is located there." For three months Van and I traveled to Arizona, Atlanta, Florida, Tennessee, and Alabama. And I testify to you that by the end of those three months, we had ministered to black and white, young and old, educated and uneducated, people with money and people with no money. In three months, we had influenced so many people to try God that it was mind-blowing!

I came to this conclusion: I am a pastor—not because I am the pastor of Pilgrim Baptist Church, but because that is what God made me. And no matter where I am, I am pastoring.

As a result of that, I believe that no matter where we are, God is on location. Wherever we are—at the mall, the gym, school, on the job—that is where God is. Wherever we are, God ought to be given the glory out of our lives, and somebody ought to see Jesus because we, as believers, are there. When I tell you that I did not need another car, more money, and that kind of thing, here is why: because I said, "If I take care of God's business, God will take care of my business." If you do the same, soon you'll start using words like "amazing" and "unbelievable" and "unimaginable" as you begin to experience God's favor in your life. You'll get more done with less effort because now you are delighting yourself in God.

Desires
(Psalm 37:4)

God then begins to give you the desires of your heart. Imagine that!

This is what happens when you are in one accord with God. God knows what you need, and God knows what you want. Simple things like, "Lord, I have a long way to go now, and I need a parking space when I get there." Once you arrive, somebody pulls out of a parking space, and you easily take that space.

Or, "Lord, I want to go visit this family, but I don't know what they need. Please give me what they need." Then you begin to share, and you find that what you talk about is exactly what they needed to hear. And they ask you, "How did you know that particular verse you just read is what we needed?" This is called *favor*.

Remember what John Knox said about ordinary people—you don't have to be on television or radio to be used by God. You don't even need a title or a particular agenda, nor do you have to be of a certain age. And you don't have to have that college degree yet. All God requires is that you spend enough time with Him to begin to have Him shape your life and your desires. And then you will begin to see supernatural things happen.

Colossians 1:28 states that what Christ is trying to do is conform you to His image. All He wants you to do is be like Him. You and I; Christ in us; the hope of glory. And, if you do that, then prayer becomes the medium by which you can live a life that is so abundant, so energized, and so meaningful that you will not be content to live any other way.

There is a beverage advertised on television that is supposed to work wonders for people with high cholesterol. Drinking it will cause the cholesterol to practically fall off. Have you seen that commercial? By comparison, when we internalize prayer the way God wants us to, all of the common desires and natural behaviors of humans—material things, gossip, envy, jealousy, judging others—will simply fall off us.

In conclusion, it becomes easier to be a giver than a receiver. Praying and being in God's presence teaches us this. There's always going to be somebody who has more than you have. You are going to have to learn to be content with what you have.

Let me tell you something else. There is always going to be somebody who is smarter than you, so you might as well learn to be satisfied with the sense that you have. There is always going to be somebody who looks better than you. As cute as you think you are, there is always someone who is going to be cuter. If you can turn one head, there is always someone who can turn two. So when you look in the mirror, just say, "I love me."

If we pray, then we will begin to be content with who we are, what we have, our abilities, and all of that. We will then begin to love one another as we love ourselves.

It all begins with prayer. In John 16:24, Jesus said, "If you ask *anything* in My name, I will do it." (paraphrased)

Once you begin spending more and more time with Him, you will see changes in your life!

Questions to Consider

1. *What is a simple definition of prayer?*

2. *Does doubt enter your mind while praying?*

3. *How can you improve your level of intimacy with God?*

2

Prayer According to Jesus—Part 1

Luke 6:12–16, Mark 6:46,
Matthew 14:23, John 6:15

And it came to pass in those days, that he went out into a mountain to pray, and continued all night in prayer to God. And when it was day, he called unto him his disciples: and of them he chose twelve, whom also he named apostles; Simon, (whom he also named Peter,) and Andrew his brother, James and John, Philip and Bartholomew, Matthew and Thomas, James the son of Alphaeus, and Simon called Zelotes, And Judas the brother of James, and Judas Iscariot, which also was the traitor. (Luke 6:12–16, KJV)

Our primary text is going to be Luke 6:12–16. Do you know why this passage is important to me, and why it interests me? Because Jesus was fully God. Yes, He was also fully human. But what impresses me, what interests me, and what gets my attention is that although Jesus is God, He takes time to pray. Now imagine that! Oftentimes the Lord will say, "I know what you are thinking. I know what you are going to do. You are not surprising Me because you are asking, just like I knew you would ask." Yet the Lord still takes time to pray to the Father, even though He knows everything. This tells me that if the Lord Jesus, who has unbroken fellowship with the Father, takes time to pray, that means you and I, sure enough, have to take time to pray. Jesus spent time with the Father in eternity, and He's going back to eternity—yet He spends time in prayer. Do you know why those of us who are not both human and divine, but only human, ought to pray? Because we do not have unbroken fellowship with God. We know that to understand God, we have to pray.

The Place of Prayer—The Mountain

The first thing we will look at is the place of prayer. Notice that Jesus goes to a mountain. The books of Matthew, Mark, Luke, and John all say that Jesus spent significant time on the mountain. Whenever Jesus really wanted to understand the Father's will, He always went to the mountain.

Now, the mountain was not like Mount Tamalpais in California—green with marked-out trails. It was more like the mountains in Arizona—just rocks that you have to go through a lot of trouble to get to. Yet Jesus always went to the mountain whenever He spent serious time in prayer with God. Why is that important?

How many of you have ever been to Israel? Israel is a hilly country with rocky terrain. But Jesus, when He gets ready to pray, goes to the mountain. What does that teach us?

1. It took effort to get there. Jesus did not just go to the mountain. He walked for miles over difficult terrain then climbed steep and jagged slopes to find a place where He could pray. In other words, that took effort. He did not just decide, "Well, I guess I will go to the mountain." He really had to plan and make preparations to get there. So Jesus goes to the mountain, and it takes great effort to get there.

2. There are fewer distractions there. Modern Christians pray with their cell phones on just in case they get a call. Modern Christians pray with their pagers on in case someone really needs to get in touch with them. Modern Christians pray with the Internet on, listening for the noise that tells they have an e-mail. Modern Christians pray with the radio tuned to talk radio. Modern Christians pray with the television on.

We are distracted, so we are not praying. Most of us cannot keep our minds on several things at once. Most of us have to focus. But Jesus decides, "If I am going to pray, I have got to put effort in it by going to the mountain. I am choosing the mountain because there will be no distractions there. I am praying; I am talking to the Father. I do not want any distractions, so I make an effort."

3. The mountain is a place of intimacy. When you go to the mountains in Israel, trust me, you are not going to be bothered by anybody else.

Nobody is going to be there but you. So the mountain is an intimate place for Jesus to spend time with God without any distractions. There He can really be with the Father one-on-one. He can cultivate intimacy. He can spend time alone talking to God—nobody but God! Jesus chose this place to be intimate with God in prayer.

4. Jesus is able to think there. Prayer includes your mind. You have to think about prayer. You don't just pray. You think about what you are going to pray about.

Now, let us review this and ask ourselves some questions.

- When you decide to pray, do you go to a special place? Does it take some effort to get there?

- Do you have to go out of your way to get to your prayer ground?

You see, here is what we often do. "Pastor, I pray in my shower. When I bathe myself, you know, I talk to God." Or, "I pray in the car, driving down Highway 101." Or, "I pray on the subway or on the bus." "I just pray as I go along."

The problem with that kind of prayer is that it is a prayer of convenience. You are attempting to pray as you are doing something else. What Jesus' example teaches us is that for us to really have intimacy with God, we have to make some effort. That is why sometimes the prayers we do on our bed may not really be prayers; it might be meditation. So, to really pray, we have got to get out of bed and make some effort to go somewhere to be alone with God. Jesus shows us that sincere prayer requires some effort. You have to get out of your comfort zone to do it.

- When you pray, are you assured of little or no distraction?

When you pray, you cut off everything; you turn off everything; you shut down everything that might distract you. This is a time when you are alone with God.

Sometimes my wife, Van, will say to me, "I am going to pray." That means, "Don't bother me." Or sometimes I will say, "I am going to have time with the Lord." And she knows not to interrupt that time. We have to make some effort to do that. Do you do that?

- Are you seeking some time of intimacy with God?

- Is that what you are really looking for?

Prayer time is not just a time to ask God for things. Are you really excited about just being in God's presence? I believe that real prayer takes place when you are just glad to be in the presence of God—not making any requests, but just glad to be in God's presence. I honestly believe that you and I will increase our prayer lives when we understand that the benefits of prayer are not asking God for anything, but just being with Him. Hanging out with the Lord in prayer is a really good use of your time.

The Practice of Prayer

We have to be sure that when we pray, we don't just ask God for lots of things and then say, "In Jesus' name, amen," and get up.

If you made thirty minutes' worth of requests, then how long should you spend listening? Thirty minutes. You cannot just rush into God's presence and say, "Lord, I need this and that, and please do this and that. Thank you." And then go. The Lord says, "Wait a minute. Hold it, hold it. I have got some things I want to say to you. What about your attitude? You have been irritable lately. I need to tell you about that. What about your spirit? You have been a little cantankerous lately. Let me tell you about that." Oftentimes you and I will not allow another human to tell us anything. So the only way for us to get information is for God to tell us directly. Spending time with God includes listening time, not just asking time.

There are some other factors to consider in the practice of prayer:

1. Time. Set a particular time to pray and spend time with God. This is how I discipline myself to pray at a certain time. Let's say I'm going to spend three hours watching a football game, and then thirty minutes going over the highlights. I might say to myself, "Okay. That is three-and-a-half hours of television. Now, how long will I spend in the word? Or how long will I spend in prayer? Or how long will I spend visiting someone? Or how long will I spend calling someone?" I never allow myself to spend more time in pleasure then I spend with God. That is my rule. Some days I do not watch television at all. Why? Because I watched two games on Sunday. That's six hours. For the rest of the week, I don't watch television because I am making up for the time spent watching the game.

You, too, have to set aside time to spend with God. It is not just going to happen. You have to plan it. Sometimes you even have to enter a certain time in your day planner—or your iPod or whatever you use—that you are going to spend in prayer. Keep that appointment with God just as you would keep an appointment with a friend or loved one.

Jesus said, "Listen. I am going to the mountain, and I am going to spend some time there." How much time did He spend? All night long. The Lord said, "On this day, I know I am not going to get any sleep because tonight I am going to the mountain." Now remember: "all night" means what? There are no lights, no company, and there may be the danger of wild animals. "But tonight I am going to spend all night in prayer. Tonight I have set aside that time." So if the Lord set aside time for prayer, how much more should you and I set aside time for nothing but prayer?

2. Place. Jesus says that when you pray, do so in a private place, like your own room (Matt. 6:6). The Lord seems to indicate in this Scripture that you and I ought to have not only a time but a place in which to pray, a place that we have designated as our altar. Remember Abraham? When he went to Bethel, he built an altar and called upon the name of the Lord (Gen. 12:8). As a believer, you need to have an altar in your home where you can say, "Now listen, this little spot right here: it may not be anything but a candle, a Bible, and a pillow, but this is my altar. I am going to spend time here with God every day."

(I've had people say to me, "Pastor, you mean to tell me that I need to pray every day? Isn't that legalistic?" My response is, "You eat five times a day! I know it's five. I can tell it's five, not three—five!")

3. Agenda. The practice of prayer also requires an agenda. This means that when I pray on Monday, for example, I am going to pray for my family. Monday is family time. Tuesday may be my time to pray for ministry leaders and their families. Wednesday may be special needs—people in the hospital, for example, or others, depending on what is going on around me. For me, Thursday is sermon preparation and praying about the will of God. Friday may be additional special needs.

Every day I have some type of agenda so that I can make sure that in a week's time, I have covered everything and everybody. I call that "intentionality." So if one of the deacons in the church asks me, "Pastor, have you been praying for me?" I can honestly say yes, because there is, in fact, a certain day that I pray for the deacons, their wives, and their children. I have learned that I have to organize my prayer time such that I have a time, a place, and an agenda.

Now, when Jesus decided to go to the mountain to spend the time in prayer, He also had an agenda.

Matthew 15:38 states that Jesus fed four thousand on one occasion, and Matthew 14:21 states that He fed five thousand on another occasion. He could see that there were some who were actually getting the word. Others were not. Some seemed hungry. Some were attentive. And for some, it went over their heads. He had been doing this in different cities throughout the Jordan Valley.

So the Lord was thinking: "How can I be sure that this is the best method for getting the word out? I don't want to just preach to mega-crowds and think that just because I have numbers, I have quality. What I need to do is take some time and spend it with God to make sure that this is the best method to get the message out."

Jesus had an agenda. He prayed all night. And guess what God told Him? "That mega-church thing? That is not it. That is not My way." He said to Jesus, "Now listen. If You are really going to get this kingdom concept down, here is what You need to do. You have to narrow the focus down. Invest Your life in a smaller number and make sure that the smaller number gets it." That is a much better methodology. Preaching to thousands is appealing and ego-stroking. It's nice to have a crowd. But God said to Jesus, "That is not how I work. Here is what You are to do."

The Results of Prayer

The wisdom that God gave Jesus as a result of Jesus praying all night long was to choose twelve disciples. That did not just come to Him. He didn't decide on His own, "I am going to choose twelve." No. The text says He did it after doing what? Spending all night in prayer! There are some things we will never get unless we talk to God about it over an extended time. Otherwise, we end up just mimicking the way everybody else has done it before.

Crowds! Everybody wants a crowd. So, let's get a crowd. How do you get a crowd? You get a crowd by telling people basically what they want to hear.

How do you get a crowd? You get a crowd by lowering the standards until there really is no high bar to try to reach.

How do you get a crowd? You get a crowd by not condemning anything and accepting everything.

How do you get a crowd? You get a crowd by giving people what they want, not what they need.

How do you get a crowd? You placate them; you satisfy them. That is how you get a crowd. But crowds do not produce disciples, and the Lord said that it is not *quantity* but *quality*. So after a night in prayer, Jesus chooses twelve disciples.

Let's look more closely at the results of prayer:

1. Wisdom. Let me say something about this that may encourage some of you. The Lord prayed all night long and only chose twelve disciples. The Lord fed four thousand; fed five thousand; and sent out seventy-two (Luke 10:1, KJV). But when He was ready to choose intimate followers, how many did he name? Twelve! The Bible states that those twelve disciples turned the world upside down. Many congregations have massive numbers but little impact.

Let us look at the text again. Often we do not read the Scripture closely, so we miss a lot. In verse 14, Simon—called "Peter" by Jesus—is the first mentioned. Peter really came to Christ as a result of Andrew, his brother. Interestingly, although Andrew is named as an apostle, the Bible doesn't tell us anything else about him other than that he brought Peter to the Lord.

James and John, who are brothers, both wrote Scripture. Peter wrote Scripture. Philip becomes an evangelist but is not known to have written anything. We never learn anything more in the Bible about Bartholomew at all.

Matthew was a sinner and a tax collector, and he wrote Scripture. Thomas is known for doubting Christ after His resurrection, but nothing else is mentioned in the Bible about him or about James, the son of Alphaeus. Simon the Zealot was a fighter and a political activist. Judas, the brother of James, also earns no other mention in the Bible.

Judas Iscariot ended up betraying the Lord. Notice that verse 16 reads, "*became* a traitor." This means that when God called Judas, he had the potential to be as strong in faith as anyone else, but he became a traitor. Somewhere along the line, he stopped believing in the Lord's work.

What does this say to us? The Lord prayed all night and then called twelve disciples. One of them betrayed him, and half of them did not accomplish anything noteworthy enough to be included in the Bible. A small remnant wrote Scripture that is still with us today.

What does that tell us? In any large group, there is a small group that is really going to do most of the work. And within that small group is a small group that is going to do the things that really last. What then do we see as one result of prayer? *Wisdom.*

There are some things that God will only tell you in prayer. You will never get to them unless you get to them on your knees … which tell us that most of us, honestly, have never, ever heard a word from God. Most of us cannot say "God told me," because we do not spend enough time with Him to hear what He is saying.

Most of us are content to have someone else go to God, get something, and then tell us what God said. We don't know if it's true or not, but we don't want to go through the effort of getting it for ourselves. That's why our popular culture lifts up so many celebrities. "Bishop So-and-So said this." "Prophet So-and-So said that." "Apostle So-and-So said this." "My radio preacher said this." "Evangelist So-and-So said that." But what did God say to you? If we have spent time in prayer, we can say, "God talked to me. I do not go to anybody else. I go to God myself."

But most of us get our information from God second-, third-, fourth-, or fifth-hand: "he said," "she said," "they said," "I felt," "I heard." Not many of us spend enough time with God to hear God. The result of not spending enough time in prayer is *lack* of wisdom.

Here is a good application. Most of our lives are the sum total of our choices. You and I make certain choices as adults, and the rest of our lives are lived trying to work out the choices that we've made. Maybe you marry someone in your twenties, and you have some children together, and you spend the next forty years trying to figure out why you married each other. The truth is that you did not pray about it.

Most of us who are single could have somebody if we prayed. We have nobody because we do not pray. Why do I say that? Most of us have a human picture of who we want. We are not going to marry anybody until we find that perfect person. He or she has to have a certain job, a certain car, a certain look, a certain complexion. Some of you say, "My perfect partner has to be light-skinned." Or, "He has to make at least six figures." Or, "She has to have a bachelor's degree and be working on her master's." You never meet anybody like that, so you are single.

Let me tell you what happens. If you start praying, fasting, seeking God, and getting God's wisdom, then God is going to say, "There she is!" Or, "There he is, right there. Right there!" Or you are having lunch in the cafeteria and the Lord says, "There he is!" And you say, "Johnny? In the rear room?" Or, "Sally? Who's an assistant to the assistant to the assistant to the assistant clerk? Her?" And then you say, "I'd rather be single, Jesus." But honestly, if we really got serious, many of us would be surprised at what God will say to us through prayer. We will get *wisdom.*

As I said, most of our lives are the sum total of our choices, and our choices, when they are not bathed in prayer, are unwise. Every concern that we have ought not to be decided until we have bathed it in prayer over and over and over again. Then, after you have prayed about it, ask God for three signs—not one, not two, but three—to make sure that it is a good decision. We get wisdom from being in prayer.

2. Confidence. This is the second result of prayer. When you come to a conclusion as a result of prayer, then you can move forward with confidence because you are sure that God has given you the okay. "You can start the business now," God says. Not based on the economy; not based on what is the apparent need. But God says, "Start it now, and I will bless it." Or God says, "Step out now and buy the house." The economy is messed up and you don't know what you are going to get, but you were in prayer and God said, "Do it now." Or you're getting ready to do it and you have all your ducks lined up and God says, "No, not now. Wait."

Wisdom, and the confidence that you get from wisdom, comes from listening to God. When you hear God say in prayer, "I do not care if the devil in hell comes to get you, you will have confidence," then you will have confidence.

"I know God told me to do it."

"You're sure?"

"Yes, I'm sure."

"Well, what about this?"

"So what?"

"What about that?"

"So what? God told me."

When God says it, it does not have to make sense to anybody but you. God said it, so do it.

I was just thinking about one of the brothers in our church. When his daughter started a business, he helped her. He had no idea that those few dollars he put in her hand would become millions. But she told him, "I believe this is of God," and he had enough confidence to say, "Go for it." Most of us want a guarantee, and we're not going to do anything until we know that there is no possibility of failure.

Let me give you a formula for success:

Risk + Responsibility = Reward

Whether it is in the spiritual realm, the secular realm, or any other realm you want to name, it is always *Risk + Responsibility = Reward*. In other words, if you want a great return, you have got to invest risk—even in prayer. You have got to ask God for the big thing, the great thing, the hard thing, the tough thing.

"You need somebody to do it, God? Here I am. Send me!"

"I will take it, Lord. You need somebody to lead the children's ministry? I will take it. You need somebody to start a hospitality committee? I will do it. Need somebody to start the Outreach Team? I will do it."

No risk, no responsibility, no reward. God is not going to say, "Well done!" if you do not do anything. Confidence!

3. Courage to face enemies or obstacles. Then courage to face inner risks and obstacles.

Most of us are looking for a good place to quit.

One January, I noticed two things about our church: people show up on the last Sunday of the year and on the first Sunday of the year. I don't know if it's superstition or what. But on the last Sunday of the year, there is a good crowd. And on the first Sunday, there is a good crowd. It's almost as if they are saying, "I want to be here on the last Sunday so God will bless me to see the first Sunday. Then I want to start out on the first Sunday for good luck."

Then about February, March, April, the weather starts changing. And the numbers start decreasing, because those people really did not have their minds made up in the first place.

Prayer will encourage you should someone come to you and say, "You cannot say this or do that," or if the devil, for instance, stands in front of you. If you pray, you will have the confidence and the courage to keep on going and see what the end is going to be.

4. Choices to live by/with. Finally, you will make some choices after prayer that you can live by and you can live with. If God tells you to start a business and that business goes bankrupt, but you know God told you to do it, you will not be discouraged. If God tells you to do something and it does not work out the way you think, God will take the failure and bless you with it. God will take what does not work out and bless it. Romans 8:28 says, "All things work together for good as long as we love God in our core."

In other words, when you get your answer in prayer, it is going to work out, no matter how it looks to you or anyone else. That is what the Lord did. Jesus went to the mountain; it was hard to get there. Jesus went there because it was a place of no distraction. Jesus had a set agenda: "Here is what I am praying about today." Then, whatever God, the Father, told Him to do, He did it. Everybody else was trying to get a crowd. But the Lord said, "Give me twelve and I will change the world." (Please note, though, that there is nothing inherently wrong with large ministries.)

I do not know what God is telling you to do. But God is telling you to do something. God is saying to you, "Invest your life in something beyond yourself. There is somebody who needs you and the contribution you can make, and no one else can make it but you." Nobody else is wired like you are to get done what God is calling you to do.

Pray long enough to determine what it is God wants you to do. Then spend the rest of your life trying to do it.

Prayer

God, we thank You for our time of study. We pray now, God, that You will hide Your word in our hearts so we might not sin against You. Bless it now in Jesus' name. Amen.

Questions to Consider

1. *How much time do you set aside for prayer each day?*

2. *Does praying all night appeal to you?*

3. *What hinders you from spending time with God?*

3

Prayer According to Jesus—Part 2

Matthew 6:5–13

Continuing our subject of prayer according to Jesus, let us add the passage about being steadfast in prayer. We are not to pray intermittently; we are to continue steadfastly, praying again and again and again. Not that God cannot hear, but it is our patience in prayer that brings fruit.

"And when you pray, you shall not be like the hypocrites, for they love to pray standing in the synagogue and on the corners of the street, that they may be seen by men. Assuredly, I say to you, they have their reward.

But you, when you pray, go into your room and when you have shut your door, pray to your Father who is in your secret place; and your Father who sees in secret will reward you openly.

And when you pray, do not use vain repetitions as the heathen do. For they think that they will be heard for their many words.

Therefore, do not be like them, For your Father knows the things you have need of before you ask him.

In this manner, therefore, pray:

Our Father which art in heaven, hallowed be thy name.

Thy kingdom come. Thy will be done in earth, as it is in heaven.

Give us this day our daily bread.

And forgive us our debts, as we forgive our debtors.

And lead us not into temptation, but deliver us from evil. For thine is the kingdom and the power and the glory forever. Amen." (Matt. 6:5–13)

I want to give you a quote and, if you do not write it down, at least try to memorize it because it sets the foundation/stage for this ministry of prayer. The quote is: "The weakest Christians on their knees who make contact with heaven are more powerful than the strongest demons in hell."

Listen again! "The weakest Christians on their knees who make contact with heaven are more powerful than the strongest demons in hell."

We are looking at the *practice* of prayer, the *pattern* of prayer, and the *power* of prayer.

In 2 Chronicles 7:14, the word "if" is used:

> If my people, which are called by my name, shall humble themselves, and pray, and seek my face, and turn from their wicked ways; then I will hear from heaven, and will forgive their sin, and will heal their land.

"If" indicates that there is a strong sense that the people of God would not pray. It is really a conditional sentence that gives us a promise worth trying to capture. "If My people [those who are called by My name] would humble themselves, seek My face, and turn from their wicked ways, then—here is the promise—I [God] will hear from heaven and heal the land."

It seems to me that if believers all over the world would take this promise from God seriously, if all of us would get together and pray in a humble and sincere way, and if all of us would turn away from wrongdoing, then God will hear, God will answer, and God will heal the land.

Every one of us has to admit that our land is ill in so many ways—spiritually, financially, emotionally. Any way we look at it, all of us must admit that our land needs some healing. Why is it, then, that we still cannot rally the people of God together—all denominations, ages, and countries—if for no other reason than that the land would be healed? It seems to me that if all of us understood that there is a need for healing, then why would all of us not commit ourselves to prayer?

Maybe we can find something of an answer in 2 Corinthians 5:7: "For we walk by faith, not by sight." Could it be that we do not try to grasp the possibilities of prayer in 2 Chronicles 7:14 because we do not truly believe that God can and will do anything about our situation? Maybe we do not have a practical faith that says, "I know that God does hear and answer prayer. I know that there is value in prayer; therefore, I give myself to it." Maybe the people of God, on a large scale, do not have confidence that God still answers prayer. If we did have confidence, we would do what? We would pray. And the very fact that we do not pray and do not give serious attention to prayer leads me to the conclusion that we truly do not have faith in prayer and, therefore, do not have faith in God.

In 2 Corinthians 10:4, we read: "For the weapons of our warfare are not carnal but mighty through God to the pulling down of strongholds" (KJV).

This text is saying that there are some strongholds, fortresses, and embankments that the enemy—the devil—has built up against us individually and collectively. There are some fortresses or strongholds that the demons, imps, and minions of hell have fortified. And, because of these strongholds, there is spiritual warfare. We have to engage the enemy in battle.

Therefore, as the Apostle Paul wrote in Ephesians 6:13, you and I must put on the whole armor of God so that we might be able to stand against the evil day. What a promise that we can, by prayer, pull down the enemy's fortresses and strongholds! Those are the very things that keep people in bondage. By prayer we can pull those things down! Wouldn't we all agree that there are a lot of people who are in bondage, who are trying to break through, but who cannot and have not? That's because we are not using this powerful weapon called prayer.

The Practice of Prayer

Jesus assumes that we will pray. It is almost as if He assumes that once you enter into a relationship with Him and have named Him Lord of your life, then you are going to give yourself over to prayer. He assumes this in giving us the Lord's Prayer—that you and I will pray.

We make it so difficult. Prayer does not have to have flowery language. Jesus says later on in the Scripture that using a lot of words won't make God hear your prayer any more clearly (Matthew 6:7). But you and I, because of religion, church, ritualism, and tradition, have made prayer such a difficult thing that most of us feel like we are not up to the task. Yet, all prayer is simply talking with God.

There is nothing highfalutin about prayer. There is nothing mystical about prayer. There is nothing difficult about prayer. You talk to God just like you would talk to any other person. That is why the word "Father" is used. You don't have to get a running start—"Now, Lord"—and then pray. Just talk to God. Tell Him "all about your troubles." Just take your burdens to the Lord and leave them there. Do not try for flowery language, a good beginning, a smooth transition, and a nice conclusion. No, just talk to Him.

He assumes that we will pray. In Matthew 6:5, Jesus says, "And when you pray," meaning that you are going to do it. In Matthew 6:6, He says, "But you, when you pray." In Matthew 6:7, He says, "And when you pray." That's three times. You know three times is a heavy emphasis. Jesus really means it. Three times He says, "When you pray."

Now, look at modern believers. "Well, I pray in the shower." "I pray en route to work." "I pray on my coffee break." "I pray in my bed before I go to sleep." "I pray during commercials of my favorite show." But Jesus assumes we understand that prayer is such a powerful weapon in our hands that you and I will make the time—not just take the time—to pray.

What has happened is that the devil has stolen prayer from us. Remember the Dr. Seuss story, *How the Grinch Stole Christmas*? The devil has stolen prayer because he knows, as I quoted earlier, the weakest Christians on their knees who make contact with heaven are more powerful than the strongest demons in hell. The devil knows that if he can keep us busy doing a lot of things that may be good, spiritual, or nice while keeping us off our knees, you and I will not be useful for the Master's work. We give hours and hours to so much other stuff.

Many years ago, I visited an elderly church member during the O. J. Simpson trial. I believe that trial lasted approximately nine months. This member would brag to me, "Pastor, that trial has been going on now for weeks!" The weeks turned into months. She boasted that she never missed a moment of the O. J. Simpson trial. Even back then, I thought, "If that saint would spend as much time in the word and prayer as she has spent watching the O. J. Simpson trial, how much farther along she would be in her spiritual life."

Let me stop and make some applications here. What do you spend most of your spare time on? What is it that you love to do that you literally spend hours doing? Now, let me ask you to compare that with the amount of time you spend in prayer. Whatever you love to do, I guarantee you that it is not nearly as useful and beneficial as prayer. If you take the number-one thing that you love to do—I don't mean sinful things; I mean just habits and hobbies—and if you make prayer the number-one thing and make the other activity the number-two thing, I guarantee you that your life will be so much better. Jesus assumes it!

The disciples said to Jesus, "Lord, teach us to pray, as John [the Baptist] also taught his disciples" (Luke 11:1). Do you know what happened? The disciples saw John modeling prayer. They saw John's followers modeling prayer. They saw the mighty things that John and his disciples did as a result of prayer. The disciples might have said, "Lord, we see what powerful men of God John's disciples are, and we know that it is directly related to prayer. So, Lord, teach us to pray, as John also taught his disciples." Jesus' response is recorded in Luke 11:2: "So He said to them, 'When you pray, say:'" and He gave them the Lord's Prayer.

Suppose you make prayer such a vital part of your life that somebody might ask you, "I notice a change in you. What is it?" Then you could say, "I am praying more." And they might say, "Teach me to pray just like you."

Jesus assumes prayer. He assumes a *when*, (Matt. 6:5–7). Jesus also assumes a *where* (Matt. 6:6): your room. The psalmist says, "He who dwells in the sacred place of the Most High shall abide under the shadow of the Almighty" (Ps. 91:1). Your room is your sacred place. It is that place that you have designated as your altar. When you get serious about prayer, go into your room, shut the door, and talk to God.

Jesus assumes *when*. Jesus assumes *where*. And Jesus also assumes *what* our prayer agenda will be. The Scripture says, "Hallowed be Your name." That is the *what* of prayer. Spend some time in prayer just praising His name.

There are so many names for God. In prayer, you can just meditate on Jehovah. You can really become a "Jehovah's Witness." If someone asks me, "Are you a witness of Jehovah?" I say, "Yes, I am."

"Oh, really? What hall do you go to?"

I say, "I go to Pilgrim Baptist."

"No, I mean, you are a Jehovah's Witness. You go to Kingdom Hall."

I say, "Yeah, I am a Jehovah's witness. I really am. I am a witness for Jehovah."

When you pray, pray in His name:

- Jehovah-Jireh (Gen, 22:14)

- Jehovah-Nissi (Exod. 17:15)

- Jehovah-Shalom (Judg. 6:24)

- Jehovah-Shammah (Ezek. 48:35)

- Jehovah El Shaddi (Gen. 17:1)

- Jehovah-tsidkenu (Jer. 23:5–8)

You could just pray in the name of Jehovah and get happy!

I am not asking God for anything but just His name. "Hallowed be Your name." In other words, when you pray, just spend some time shouting about His name. Just His name! You are not trying to get something. You are just caught up in His name. "Hallowed be Your name." That is the *what* of prayer.

There might be another reason why we do not pray: because the *what* of prayer also is, "Thy kingdom come." Not now!

I had a dear person in my life who was thirty-nine years old. She was going through a serious illness and also was about to graduate from college. One day she said to me, "Larry, I know I am going to heaven, but I sure do not want to go before I get my college degree."

The reason that we do not enter into that kind of prayer is that we really are not ready for His kingdom. As I said, "I want to go to heaven, but not now." We want to go to heaven, but we do not want to die.

So when you pray, Jesus says to begin with, "Hallowed be My name! Make My name special." Then the *what* of prayer is to say, "Lord, I want Your kingdom to come. I want Your rule to be realized in my life. I want the world to be like the kingdom of heaven. That is what I want." Not pleasure—but kingdom rule. Not the rule of the flesh, but the rule of the Spirit. "Thy kingdom come." That is what I want. God's rule.

You cannot pray for God to rule unless you allow Him to rule you. You cannot pray, "Thy kingdom come," and remain selfish. You cannot pray, "Thy kingdom come," and want to do what you want when you want to do it. When you pray, "Thy kingdom come," that means you are saying to God, "I am no longer in control. From now on, You call the shots in my life. When You say 'Go,' I will go. When You say 'Stop,' I will stop. When You say, 'Speak,' I will speak. I am no longer my own."

In Philippians 3:10–11, Paul said, "… that I may know Him and the power of His resurrection, and the fellowship of His sufferings, being conformed to His death, if, by any means, I may attain to the resurrection from the dead." Paul is saying, "I want the same power that raised up Jesus to flow through my life." Imagine that! That same power that resurrected Jesus would flow in your life every day. Every day! Think about it! The only way you can pray, "Thy kingdom come," is if you have that same attitude. In Phil. 3:8, Paul said "I count all things but garbage." Actually, the word he uses is "manure"—dung! All of my achievements, all of my accomplishments, and all of my accumulations are just manure. Dung! I would give it all up and I would set it on the side for the ecstasy of knowing Christ.

You cannot pray for long without coming to realize that you cannot keep doing what you are doing and keep praying. It is been said that sin would drive you *to* God or sin would drive you *from* God. But you cannot have both. You cannot have sin and God. It seems to me that many have chosen sin over God.

Jesus assumes it, saints. The *when*, the *where*, and the *what*. "Hallowed be thy name. Thy kingdom come." And here it is: "Thy will be done." Do you know what the word "will" means? W-a-n-t. God's will becomes what you want. All I want is to do God's will.

Dr. Martin Luther King, Jr., said that he knew he was going to die. In his famous "I've Been to the Mountain Top" speech, he said, "Like anybody, I would like to live a long life. Longevity has its place. But I'm not concerned about that now. I just want to do God's will." Look at the changes he made.

The devil has manipulated us into thinking that if we do decide to do God's will—boring! Cannot have anymore fun! I am going to be left out of all the action! I will not be part of the "in" crowd any more!

But just the opposite is true. Do God's will, and your life will have meaning, purpose, and passion. You will have joy, favor, and the blessing of God in your life. You will be confident, reassured, strong, and courageous. You will be able to face the mighty foe and win the battle because you are in God's will. When you are out of God's will, you are timid, weak, weary, sad, negative, envious, and jealous. Which would you rather be?

The Pattern of Prayer

In Matthew 6:5, Jesus said, "Do not be like the hypocrite." The word "hypocrite" means "pretender." Do not pretend that you are spiritual. Do not pretend that you are sanctified. Do not pretend that you love God. Do not pretend that you are Holy Ghost-filled. Do not be a pretender.

The word "hypocrite" comes from the Greek word meaning "actor"—someone acting out a role on a stage. Jesus said over and over again that the scribes and Pharisees were hypocrites (Matt. 6:2, 5, 16; Matt. 23:27, Luke 6:42, Luke 11:44). They were pretenders. And let me tell you this: it takes the same amount of energy to do it right as it does to pretend. The same amount of energy! It takes the same amount of effort to pretend that you love as it does to actually love. It takes the same amount of energy to live a committed life as it does to live an uncommitted life. Stop being a hypocrite! Stop pretending! Use your time, talent, and treasure well. Do it right. Jesus said, "Do not be like the hypocrite. Do not pretend like the heathen, for they think they will be heard for their many words (Matt. 6:7)." He was describing those who babbled publicly in the synagogue or on the street corners—all in front of crowds.

One historian, Josephus, said that the scribes and Pharisees would not pray in public until the crowd grew to a sizable number. This reminds me of a preacher who had become so famous that he drew great crowds. He got so caught up in his ability to draw a crowd and in what they were saying about him that he said, "I will not preach unless there are at least five hundred in attendance. I will not stand and take a text unless there are at least five hundred to hear what I have to say."

Also, it is not about the volume. Sometimes we get loud. "Now, Lord!" You are not heard because of your volume. God is not hard of hearing.

Sometimes we pray on and on and on, like the Energizer Bunny. Several years ago, a little four- or five-year-old boy with boundless energy, came to the altar. One of the associate ministers was praying. This associate went on and on and on and on. I guess he wanted to preach and did not get a chance to, so he thought he would get it all out in his prayer. He went on and on and on and on. I mean, he kept going on. And then, the little boy—and I was right there listening—the little boy got up and looked at his mom and said, "Mama, that is the longest prayer I ever did hear!"

Sometimes I have heard prayers go on and on. People come to the altar and after the right amount of time, they say, "Amen." Sometimes somebody has to look over and wake the person up because he or she has gone to sleep. Prayer ought not to be so long as to bore someone to sleep. What Jesus is saying is that we are not heard for our volume, and we are not heard for the longevity of our prayers. Pray from your heart. That is all that is required. He also says that in the scribes' and Pharisees' pattern of prayer, they are heard by man, and that is their payoff. They have gotten their reward (Matt. 6:1).

The question is: when we pray, are we trying to get a human pat on the back or a heavenly pat on the back? I have heard deacons get up and say, "Thank you for that prayer." "Good prayer." "Good prayer." "Good prayer." "Great prayer." We do not know if it was a great prayer unless the Lord says, "Great prayer. Great prayer. Great prayer."

I am sure that all of us have been to services where the spirit gets high and the deacon or preacher starts praying and we go along with it by saying, "Say it, Reverend; say it, Deacon; pray on; uh-huh; that's it; yeah." And the more we urge him on, the longer he prays. Sometimes we want to say, "I wish you would stop!" We are encouraging him. All he cares about is his long prayer.

When you pray, are you looking for a humanly pat or a heavenly pat? Matthew 6:5 says, "They have their reward." After those long, flowery prayers, full of language that sounds so good, when you're finished—that's it.

There was a mother in our church years ago who said, "Reverend, a lot of these prayers are just stuck up around the ceiling and they have never gotten to heaven. When you tear this church down, they are going to find prayers up on the roof that never made it." Prayers are stuck up on the ceiling!

So we ought not to pray to be heard. I think when someone prays, we are encouraged; we are privileged to overhear the prayer as the one praying talks to God. The audience is not us. The audience is God. That is the practice of prayer and the pattern of prayer. Stormie Omartian captures my sentiment concerning the pattern of prayer with a compelling observation. "Far too often prayer becomes a complicated issue for me. In fact, there can seem to be so many aspects to it that many people become intimidated. They fear that they can't pray well enough, or long enough, or eloquent enough."[2] Many people become so frustrated with the "how" of prayer that they end up not praying at all.

The Power of Prayer

What gives prayer its power? *Jesus knows our needs.* That is encouraging. He says our heavenly Father knows what we need before we ask Him (Matt. 6:8). He already knows.

What is the power of prayer? When you and I pray, we enter into the presence of God, and we discover that by being in God's presence and listening, God wants us to ask more than we want to tell Him our needs. God is not reluctant. He is not saying, "Well, I'm just going to stand here and wait until they have prayed long enough and hard enough and have really sweated over it. Then I will answer." No. He knows your needs. There is something in the asking that benefits us. He wants us to get in the habit of asking—perhaps so we can come to really understand that He is our provider.

Years ago, when my mom was living in the South, she bought a deep freezer. When bread was on sale for three loaves for $1, Mom would buy extra and place the extra bread in the freezer. I often used to wonder as a kid, "Why do I have to pray for my daily bread when we have several loaves in the freezer?" Later on, when I was older, my mom said, "I want you to learn how to pray for bread as if there is none. If you learn to pray for bread as if there is none, you will always have some."

Jesus knows your needs. He knows the needs of the single sister or brother. He really knows your heart. God wants you to love Him before you love anyone else. If you do not love Him, when you get the one that you really want, your love for Him will fall by the wayside. I have seen that more than once.

You want that house of your own. Well, it is not that you cannot do it, but first, make Him your shelter. Make Him your habitation. Make Him your dwelling place. I am convinced, and I say this often, that if you take care of God's business—and God's business really belongs to Him—God will take care of your business. He knows our needs.

Provision—Bread

"Give us this day our daily bread" (Matt. 6:11). That is our substance. I believe we are in the midst of a recession, and I thought about this the other day when we did the sermon on trusting God through a famine. I believe that the word for all of us, and a word that we ought to carry on, is this: we ought to trust God and not begin to hedge on what we do for God, thinking that it's wise if we hold back something for a rainy day. "Seek ye first the kingdom of God and his righteousness; and all these things shall be *added* unto you" (Matt. 6:33). So do not ever think that you can hold back from God and prosper. You cannot.

Pardon—Forgiveness

Not only does Jesus know our need for provision, but notice also that He knows our need for pardon. Matthew 6:12 reads, "Forgive us our debts [our trespasses, our sins, our iniquities] as we forgive our debtors" (KJV). The idea is that we ought to be excited about forgiving those who have sinned against us so that God will get excited about forgiving us.

Forgiveness is one thing that we, as believers, have such a hard time with. "You do not know what he has done." "You do not know what she has done." "I have never been hurt like he hurt me." "You do not know what they put me through, and I just cannot forgive them." We do not realize what we are saying. The Bible says, in Matthew 6:14–15, "For if ye forgive men their trespasses, your heavenly Father will also forgive you: But if ye forgive not men their trespasses, neither will your Father forgive your trespasses" (KJV). A lot of us who think we are forgiven are really not forgiven as long as there are others whom we have not forgiven.

Protection—Temptation

"Lead us not into temptation, but deliver us from evil" (Matt. 6:13, KJV). The word "evil" is really an adjective—deliver us from the *evil one*. It is not evil as a *thing*, but the evil *one*. What Jesus is saying is, "Do not allow us to be brought into a place where the devil can tempt us." Because we are but flesh, we are prone to give in. The psalmist in Psalm 103:14 wrote, "He remembers that we are dust" (NKJV). You and I do not want to allow ourselves to get in the proximity of the evil one because we are no match for him. I do not care how strong you are, you cannot deal with the devil. Only God can. So the prayer Jesus told us to pray is, "Keep us from the evil one."

I often say that it is not surprising that the devil stays so close to us, but it is surprising how close we want to keep him to us. Many of us hang around far too near the devil's influence. Many of us know there are things—and people—that will keep us from God; but instead of saying no, we still hang out with them. The truth is that we will never become all that God would have us be until we would rather be with God than with some of the people we spend time with. We get so caught up in being around certain people that we forsake being around God. Then we often wonder why we are not growing as we would like to.

Praise

Lastly, Jesus said, "For Yours is the kingdom and the power and the glory forever" (Matt. 6:13, NKJV). But you cannot translate that properly into English. In the original language, that word is a *shout*! So when Jesus said this, He was really in a high pitch of praise. He is saying, "*Thine* is the kingdom. *Thine* is the power. *Thine* is the glory. From now on!" He closes His prayer with a shout.

When you and I *really* pray, the result will always be praise. After you've really spent time with God, when you get off your knees, there is always some joy. There is always a sense of exaltation and exultation when you are in God's presence. You cannot pray and commune with God, then get up and still be sad. No! That is a contradiction. When you are in the King's presence, there is joy, peace, and happiness.

This is prayer according to Jesus. Remember the quote from the beginning: "The weakest Christians on their knees who make contact with heaven are more powerful than the strongest demons in hell."

Questions to Consider

1. *Do you really believe God knows your needs?*

2. *Do you take every need to God?*

3. *What has been the result?*

4

God's Prayer Challenge
to His People

2 Chronicles 7:14

At the end of our last session, a lovely lady asked me, "Listen, Pastor, I am enjoying the study, but before we get too far into it, can you give us some 'how-tos'? I am new to prayer and I really do not know a lot about it."

I would like to go back to a basic passage and give us some how-tos, and I want to make it simple so that we understand that prayer is everybody's business. If I only make one contribution, I want to make this one: prayer is everybody's business.

I said in the last chapter: "The weakest Christians on their knees who make contact with heaven are more powerful than the strongest demons in hell."

In other words, brothers and sisters, I want you to understand this: you do not have to be perfect to pray. I want you to understand that you do not have to have every "i" dotted and every "t" crossed to get in touch with heaven. You can have some things that still afflict you, and yet you still can make a difference in your prayer life.

I want us to dispel this idea that there are only a certain number of people who can pray or that there is a certain person who is more prayerful than you. Let us dispel that myth. Let us be some myth-busters. Anybody who is saved and knows the Lord can contact heaven. And, it does not matter if you pray for only one minute. That 60-second prayer might move the hand of God. I want you to know that your prayer matters. In the economy of God, your prayer *does* make a difference.

I want to go back to some basic things. Christ is in the Old Testament. I have heard it said that the Old Testament is "Christ concealed," and the New Testament is "Christ revealed." In the Old

Testament (Gen. 14:18), Abraham met a person called Melchizedek, the king of Salem. The writer of Hebrews says that Melchizedek had no beginning, no end, and no parent (Heb. 7:3). Melchizedek in the Old Testament is what we would call the "pre-incarnate Christ." Don't think that you have to wait until you get to the River Jordan to meet Jesus. Jesus is in the Old Testament. If you do not understand the Old Testament, you really will not understand the New Testament. This modern idea that there is nothing of value spiritually but what is in the New Testament is not only false teaching, it is heresy. It is heresy because Psalm 23 can bless us as well as John 14 can.

2 Chronicles 6 is the background we are going to march from, and then we are going to 2 Chronicles 7:14. God challenges those who know the Lord to pray. His challenge to you is that if you pray, something will happen. There is no such thing as unanswered prayer. Every prayer that is prayed in faith is answered. Every prayer! God does not leave any believer's prayer unanswered.

We have to be insistent enough to know what the answer is from God. You cannot be looking for a certain answer with such enthusiasm that you miss the answer that God is giving you. God has more sense than we have. God has been around longer than we have. Therefore, we must acknowledge that God may not answer our prayers when we want Him to, and that only He knows how to best answer our prayers.

Everything we ask God for is not necessarily what we might need at that time. Since God is sovereign, He has the right of refusal. If God says no, you still have to say, "Thank you!" with as much enthusiasm as if He had said yes. If God says no to you, guess what? That is really yes. It is the yes you needed, even though it is not the yes that you wanted.

Solomon

Solomon, according to the Scriptures, was the wisest person who ever lived—as long as he kept his walk current with God. The Bible says that not only was Solomon the wisest, he also was the richest person ever to live in his time. Many have estimated that, by today's standards, Solomon would have been richer than Larry Ellison, CEO of Oracle Corporation, and Warren Buffet combined. When you read 2 Chronicles and look at what Solomon possessed and how God blessed him, you realize that God never had a problem with giving Solomon material things—as long as Solomon valued wisdom more than material things.

God is waiting for you to love the giver more than the gift. Solomon was wise. He probably lived to be in his mid-fifties. Tradition says that by the time Solomon died, he was somewhat mentally disturbed because he allowed what God gave him to be more valuable than the God who gave those things to him. In Ecclesiastes 2, Solomon ended up literally losing his mind trying to chase the wind. He came off saying, "Everything is vanity if you do not have God."

Solomon's words found in 2 Chronicles 6:40 would save us all a lot of trouble if we would heed them. Solomon asked God to listen to his prayer and answer it. Solomon learned to make prayer his priority. Making prayer our priority would save us a lot of trouble, because many of us waste a lot of time chasing the wind and vanity. And once we catch what we're after, we're like a dog chasing a car. When a dog actually catches up with a car, what is he going to do with it? When we catch what we are after, we are going to say, "Why?"

Prayer Is What Prompted the Promise

2 Chronicles 7:14 says, "If my people, which are called by my name, shall humble themselves, and pray, and seek my face, and turn from their wicked ways; then will I hear from heaven, and will forgive their sin, and will heal their land (KJV)."

The promise that God gives in 2 Chronicles 7 is really a prayer that Solomon prayed in 2 Chronicles 6. God is literally saying back to Solomon everything that Solomon said to Him. That is a good way to get your prayers answered. Start praying the things that God has already promised you. Find out what His promises are. I've heard it said that there are more than eight hundred thousand promises in Scripture. You can start praying the promises and receive more than you could ever imagine!

Here is the promise: "Then Solomon stood before the altar of the LORD in the presence of all the assembly of Israel, and spread out his hands" (2 Chron. 6:12, NKJV). The spreading of hands in the Old Testament is a posture of prayer. The people did not always close their eyes, but the spreading of hands, or the lifting of the hands, was a posture of prayer. In verses 12 and 13, we are told that Solomon had made a bronze platform five cubits long, five cubits wide, and three cubits high and had set it in the midst of the court. He stood on it, knelt down on his knees before all the assembly of Israel, and spread out his hands toward heaven.

In the last chapter, I said that you ought to have a designated room for prayer. Solomon literally built a platform that was high enough so all the people of Israel could see him praying. He wanted a visible demonstration. He wanted something that could be seen. He wanted to be seen as a man of prayer. I think it is a wonderful thing sometimes to pray with the door to your room open, so that your children can see you praying. Let them see, and let them hear you calling out their names before the Lord so they know that anywhere they go, prayer has them covered. Prayer ought to be secret to God, but every now and then, you ought to open the door and let your children hear you say, "Now, Lord, as they go out tonight, they say they are going one place, but God, You know that they might say one thing and do another. So Jesus, go with them. And Lord, if they have got a taste for something that they ought not to be tasting, take the taste out of their mouths." That is how the old folks pray—you all know about that.

My mother prayed that prayer one time for me. You know, I am sorry to admit it, but I started drinking when I was about fifteen years old. My mother prayed, and she prayed a long time. Her prayer really did not get answered until I was about twenty-two. But she prayed for seven years. Honestly. One night, at the age of twenty-two, I was at a party drinking, and I looked down into the cheap bourbon liquid called "Seagram's Seven," and I saw a cross. Of course, I continued drinking, but I did see it! I said to myself, "That has got to be a reflection, like the light." I continued drinking, but about two years later, I changed. After nine years! So prayer, in 2 Chronicles 6:12–13, is what prompts the promise in 2 Chronicles 7:14.

Praise Seals the Promise

Notice in 2 Chronicles 6:14 that *prayer* and *praise* go together:

And he said, "LORD God of Israel, there is no God in heaven or on earth like You, who keep Your covenant and mercy with Your servants who walk before You with all their hearts." (NKJV)

Before you ask God for anything, you should spend adequate time praising Him for what He has already done. In other words, you want to coat your asking with thanking. You want to make sure that thanksgiving is a large part of what you do when you pray. Praising God is, as I like to say, what is "going to get it when you get it."

Prayer prompts the promises of God, and praise seals the promise. Paul said, "Make your request known unto God with thanksgiving (Phil. 4:6)." In other words, when you thank God in advance for the answer, it means you believe that you are going to receive what you ask for. "I want to thank You, Lord, for the healing that I am going to receive. I want to thank You that when I come out of this surgery and wake up, the first thing on my lips will be 'Thank You.' Lord, I promise You that when [not if—mind your language], You heal me, I am going to be more committed than I am now, and I am going to be careful to give Your name all the praise, honor, and glory. And if anybody asks me how I made it through, I am going to be glad to tell them that He is my healer, my doctor."

So, prayer prompts the promise, and praise seals the promise.

Promises

Let's look at the promises. When you know the promises of God, you can pray intelligently because you can ask for what He has promised. Let us just walk through God's promises. 2 Chronicles 7:14 makes sense when we look at 2 Chronicles 6.

2 Chronicles 6:22—Sin. When we sin and come into His house and confess it, God promises us that He will forgive us. Watch this! When we come into Your house and confess our sin, You promise us that You will forgive us. That statement presupposes that you and I will sin. I do not mean any harm, but when we begin to say things like, "I thank God that I am saved and sanctified and filled with the Holy Ghost and with fire, and have not sinned all day, and that You have kept me, not against my will, but in my will," that is what I call "flowery words of nothingness." The only way that you can go all day and not sin is if you have a list of only certain sins—smoking, drinking, lusting—and you make sure you don't do any of those. But, of course, there are others not on the list that you might do.

Matthew 15:19 says that the heart is secretly wicked. Let me tell you something: most of the sin that you do you are not even aware of. Psychologists tell us that there are more than ten thousand thoughts that go through the human mind in one day, and we are not conscious of most of them. So there is a lot of sin that is registered in heaven that you do not even know you are guilty of. The things we dismiss—"I have been waiting to tell her off, and I finally did. I want to thank God for the strength to do that." We don't understand that that is pride and arrogance. There are some sins that can send you jail, but there are more sins that can send you to hell, and much of the time that is unseen stuff.

Jesus assumes—He postulates, if you will—that all of us will sin. 1 John 1:9 says, "If we confess our sins, he is faithful and just to forgive us our sins, and to cleanse us from all unrighteousness." This does not mean, brothers and sisters, that we should go out and sin willfully. Being a Christian does not mean that we are sinless. It means that we ought to sin less. But you are still going to sin. Now, it ought not to be the same thing you were doing back in 1964. It ought to be something different. We should all have grown to where we still sin, but not by doing the same sin. If we are still doing the same thing we were doing when we got saved thirty years ago, then we have problems. The sin ought to change.

2 Chronicles 6:24—Defeat. When we are defeated and come into the house, then give us victory in the midst of defeat. Sometimes on the road of life, you are going to find yourself down. Every now and then, the mine that Satan sets under your foot is going to go off. He will not miss everyone. Sometimes you are going to get caught in the shrapnel that the devil launches. When you have been defeated that week, do not come to church acting like everything is all right. "Yes, Lord, I am lifting my hands up, but I have been down all week. I barely made it. When I am defeated, give me victory."

2 Chronicles 6:26—Nature. "When natural disasters happen—tsunamis, earthquakes, floods, gasoline spills—when those happen, and I come to your sanctuary, God bless."

2 Chronicles 6:28—Provision. "When famine, recession, or inflation comes; when things are really going badly; when I come to Your house and my money is funny and my change is strange and I do not know how I am going to make it, but I make it to Your house, please, God, *provide.*"

Do you get the impression that Solomon is saying that no matter what happens, no matter what is going on, "I was glad when they said unto me, 'Let us go into the house of the LORD'" (Psalm 122:1)? This means that no matter what is going on in your life, you have to make your way to church. Feeling good or not—still come. Money or not—still come. Hurt and depressed—still come. Whatever—still come. The sanctuary is where God promises to meet us. How many can testify that you have come to church not feeling too well, but by the time of the benediction, your soul was happy?

God really wants us to always make church a part of our lives. I know of some believers who, whenever their relatives come to town for a couple of weeks, say, "Pastor, I won't be here the first and second Sunday in March. My relatives are coming from the country, and they have never been to California. My relatives told me, 'Whatever you do, we're not going to church, because we always go to church. So when we come to California, we want to have a good time.'" Others tell me, "Pastor, we won't be here; we will be entertaining." It is amazing what we will do for people and what we will not do for God.

If you come to visit me on a Sunday morning, I am going to church. (I did not just start this when I became a pastor; I have always been like this.) If you decide to sleep in, that is your business. But I am going. I will get back when I get back. You work around my schedule. And in California, nothing is happening until noon or 1:00 PM, anyway. The wine tasting does not start until 2:00 PM. You've got time to go to church, get some advanced forgiveness, and then go on.

2 Chronicles 6:29—Inclusive. "Whatever prayer, whatever supplication is made ... " By whom? "By anyone, or by all."

"When each one knows his own burden and his own grief, and spreads out his hands to this temple ... " Do you see that? If people at any time come into Your house and spread their hands out and tell You about their grief and their burden, God promises in advance that He is going to heal their grief and lift their burden. That gives all of us the sense that when we come to the Lord's house, we ought to come with some sense of excitement, some sense of expectation, and some sense of anticipation. I know God is going to do something—not because it is a particular Sunday; not because the pastor is preaching—but God has promised me that whatever I am going through or whatever I am dealing with, if I could just make my way to the house of God, that is all I need to do. Just let me get there.

Sometimes Sunday cannot come fast enough. I just want to get there. Sometimes, honestly, if I just come in and see the congregation there, I do not have to preach. There are some Sundays when I could just stand up and say, "Thank you all for coming. God bless you. Let us go home." I just want to see everyone. If I can just make it to the house of the Lord and see the saints! We all come in praising God. Excited! Already, that makes me feel good; already, I feel blessed just being in God's house.

God is saying, "These promises are yours in advance." Before you even get to the sanctuary, God has your promise already wrapped with your name on it. My God! Should we not come to church differently knowing that whatever our need is, God already knows it?

We just come in and say, "Okay, I will watch." When the choir sings, we read the bulletin. When someone is praying, half of us are looking around. I did that one Sunday. I guess the Lord or somebody said, "Look up. Look around." Half the folks were looking at me! I saw what that little boy saw when everyone bowed their heads and closed their eyes. Saints do not close their eyes anymore. Honestly. Go ahead and pick a Sunday when they are doing an altar call and kind of ease up and look around. You will find half the congregation looking at you.

There was a time that, when people prayed, they closed their eyes. Maybe people are scared. I don't know. Maybe we are living in dangerous times and people don't want to close their eyes. "I have got to watch my purse," or something. Maybe someone can tell me why.

2 Chronicles 6:34—War. Even in times of war, God will come in and, whether the war is going on in Iraq or Afghanistan or wherever, if we come and pray, He will still hear our prayers and wars will cease. David says, "He makes foes to cease and fears to cease" (Psalm 34). He makes wars to cease. Our God can actually cease wars. But it might be that we are really not asking God to cease the war because the war is profitable for a lot of us.

I do not want to get political, but let me just tell you that the war in Iraq and Afghanistan is like the war in Vietnam. It has little or nothing to do with democracy. Among the Arabs—descendants of Ishmael—democracy is the last thing on their minds. Genesis 16 says that Ishmael shall be a man of war. So, honestly, it's a nice gesture, but there will be no such thing as a permanent peace in the Middle East. It is not about democracy. It is about other things. It is about economics. But if wars are going on, the saints should come together and pray.

2 Chronicles 6:36–39—Repentance. The one thing we want to do when we come to the house of God is to come with repentance. Always be willing to turn from something and turn to God.

2 Chronicles 6:41–42—The Promise Is Repeated. That is the background of 2 Chronicles 7:14. Now let us turn to that verse itself.

Everything that is in 2 Chronicles 7:14 that God is going to give is actually the result of a prayer that Solomon prayed in 2 Chronicles 6. Many of us may never have made that connection between Chapter 6 and Chapter 7.

Chapter 7 is God saying to Solomon, "Everything that you have asked Me for I am going to do." Everything—not one thing. Remember, Solomon was not perfect. He had some issues. But everything that he asked God for, God did.

2 Chronicles 7:14. Let us look at this passage. It says, "If my people." Now, stop there. In Scripture, "if" always introduces a conditional sentence, as it does in English. "If my people." The possibility exists that they are not going to pray. That is the condition. Now, if they do, here is what is going to happen. God put "if" here because the possibility exists that no praying is going to be done. We all know you can get more Christians to a business meeting then you can to a prayer meeting.

Even though we know that prayer is what moves the hand of God, still we do not do it. Even though we understand, as John Wesley said, that "God does nothing except in answer to prayer," still we do not do it.

Most of us are crisis prayers. The only time God really hears from us with some sincerity is during a time of crisis. When our backs are against the wall and there is no way out, talk about some praying! When all hope is gone, when our battle is about to be lost, we can get in touch with God. And, as with the children of Israel, God answers—He delivers. Then, you know what we do? We go right back to our normal activities.

If—Condition for Believers. "If" is a condition for the believer. All of this is based on conditions—based on Chapter 6, and fulfilled in Chapter 7. If you pray, if you do it, He is going to make some promises. Again, remember that this is inclusive, as we saw in 2 Chronicles 6:29—anybody, anytime, anywhere, for any reason, can get in touch with God. So "if" is the believer's condition; if you pray, some things are going to happen. But you have to pray.

I am going to give you three things I discovered during my three-month sabbatical that are conditions to really getting in touch with God. These are all words that begin with "s," so they are easy to remember.

First, the believer must *saturate* himself or herself in *Scripture*. Your prayers become more powerful when you pray God's word back to Him. Even before you pray, take some time to saturate your life in Scripture. Oftentimes, my prayers seem to be more effective when I read Scripture before I begin to talk to God. So, if you really want a "how to," *saturate* yourself in *Scripture*.

Second, the believer also must saturate his or her life in the Spirit. The believer must literally say to the Holy Spirit, "Fill my mind, and fill my heart." John 7:38 says, "He that believeth on me, as the scripture hath said, out of his belly shall flow rivers of living water." Saturate your life with Scripture. Saturate your life in the Spirit.

Third, the believer must *saturate* his or her life with *singing*. With singing—with singing!

Let me tell you my routine in the morning. When I first get up—and I don't always do it all in the same order—but sometimes I have five or six songs that I listen to that really encourage me. That takes about thirty minutes. After the songs, I read the Scriptures for approximately thirty minutes. For the next thirty minutes, I saturate myself in the Holy Spirit. Then I spend another thirty minutes in prayer. That is how I start my day. The first two hours of my day are spent getting in touch with God. So those are the three things: (1) *Scripture,* (2) *Spirit,* and (3) *singing.*

Humble—condition for the heart. Now, "if" is the condition for the believer. The condition for the heart is: humility. Humble yourself. "If my people would humble themselves … " That means they are getting lower. No pride. No arrogance. No conceit. No contempt.

Back in the day, we did not have a lot of things to do to have fun. So one of the things we used to do was get a broom and go under it. That was called "Limbo." We would play some music, and we would see how low we could go. We did not have any toys. We had to use a broom. We would see who could go the lowest. See how low you can go before you pray. Humility! Matthew 23:12 says that "whoever exalts himself will be humbled, and he who humbles himself will be exalted" (NKJV). The way up is down. Humility!

Pray—condition for access. Humble yourself, and then pray. That is the condition of access. At almost any Web site—Yahoo, Google, iTunes—to access your account, you have to have a password. Log in; password. Your password to God, or your access to God, is prayer. That is how you get in touch with Him. As the song says, have a little talk with Jesus and tell Him about your trouble. He will do what? Hear your faintest cry, He will answer by and by and make it right.

Seek My face—condition for consecration. Notice that God says, "Seek My face." That is the condition for consecration. There are lots of studies of how to really get in God's face. There is a saying now, in gang language, that if you "diss" me or get in my face, I will smoke you. The idea is that you do not get too close to anyone. "Get out of my face." They will go for you if you get in their face. But what God says is just the opposite. "Guess what? I want you to get in My face. I want you to get all up in my Mug [youth slang]." God says, "Get in My face. Get in front of Me. I will hear, and I will answer. Just get all up in My grill. Come on. Get in My grill, and I will answer."

You know what a "grill" is? Not a George Foreman grill. "Grill" means what? Face, yeah. You all need to get out on the street. You have been in church. You better get out there in the street and see what is going on out there.

Turn from wicked ways—condition for repentance. Turn from what? "Wicked ways." That is repentance. Every time you and I go to God, there is always something that we need to turn from. Do not get it twisted. That is why the Bible says you cannot ever go to God and say, "I thank you, God. I am not like them. I do this and I do that" (Luke 18:11, NKJV). What does the Bible say? He went down on his knees the same way he came. But the publican, the sinner, beat his breast, smote himself, and would not even look up to heaven. He just said, "Lord, have mercy on me, a sinner." Jesus said, "That man went down justified and made right" (Luke 18:13–14, NKJV).

You cannot go to God and tell Him how good you have been. You have to go to God and tell Him how much you need Him. "I am bankrupt and busted without You, God. I need You, and I don't even know how much wrong I have done. But You know. So before we transact any prayer business, the first thing You need to do is to clean me up. Just start out right there. Clean me up! And if I think I haven't done anything, clean me twice, because I know it isn't right."

Hear from heaven—condition for consecration. Here is the condition for the answer:

- *If*—condition for the believer
- *Humble*—condition for the heart
- *Pray*—condition for access
- *Seek My face*—condition for consecration
- *Turn from wicked ways*— condition for repentance
- *Hear from heaven*—condition of the answer

He did not say you "might" hear from heaven. Notice that in these verses, everything on the side of the believer is a condition. It is an "if." But when it comes from God, there is an assurance. There is no "if" when it comes to God— No "if" at all. When God says, "You are going to hear from heaven," that means you are going to hear from heaven. No doubt about it—it is going to happen. You are going to hear, and that's not all.

These all start with "h": *Hear* from heaven. *Heal* your sin. And then *heal* the land.

Heal their sin/heal the land. I have to ask you: is the land sick? Or is the land healed? If the land is sick and getting worse, then it might not be the fault of the sinner. It might be lying at the feet of the saints. If AIDS is ravaging our community; if unwed motherhood and fatherhood is ravaging our community; if we have hundreds, thousands, even a couple of million people on parole and in jail, then it might be laid at the feet of the believers. It is not the world that God calls to give an account. He does not say, "If the sinner," but, "If my people." As the world is getting worse, it is more a condemnation of the saint than it is of the sinner, because it tells us de facto that we are not praying.

In every great revival and every great awakening known to us, there are two things: it is headed by lay people, and it is started by prayer. There has never been a revival started by preaching. Never! The great awakenings of the eighteenth century and the revivals all over Africa have all started in prayer meetings. A song has never started a revival. A sermon has never started a revival. Revivals have always been ignited by prayer. That is why He says, "Can my people do these things? Then I will do some things."

We have never had this many people consistently talking about prayer. So now, do two simple things:

1. Make a list of three people—one could be a family member, one a coworker, one a friend. I want you to make a list of three people, and then begin to pray for them regularly.

2. If the Lord gives you an opportunity to minister to one of those three, be ready and have something to say. Pray about who you need to have on your list.

Take three people and begin every day to make intercession for those three. Then, if God gives you the opportunity, be able to give an account for why you have the faith that you have.

Questions to Consider

1. Do you agree that our land needs healing?

2. *Do you believe that the promises in 2 Chronicles 7:14 are valid today?*

3. *Why is healing not taking place?*

5

The Prayer Focus

Matthew 9:36-38

But when He [who is He? Jesus] saw the multitudes, He was moved with [with what? compassion] compassion for them, because they were weary and scattered, like sheep having no shepherd. Then He said to His disciples, "The harvest truly is plentiful, but the laborers are few. Therefore pray the Lord of the harvest to send out laborers into His harvest." (Matt. 9:36–38, NKJV)

Let us talk about the prayer focus. Many are concerned about the how-tos of prayer, but let us not lose the focus of prayer. We can learn the particulars of prayer. We can pray a prayer of intercession; we can pray a prayer of adoration; we can pray a prayer of forgiveness; we can pray a prayer of sympathy and empathy; we can pray a prayer of praise; and we can pray a prayer of thanksgiving. But the focus of prayer is not those items. The focus of prayer needs to be *people*.

It may seem like a simple thought but, oftentimes, if we were to record our prayers and the prayers of others, we would discover that most of our prayers are not people-centered. We pray about situations. We pray about needs. We pray about wants. We pray about desires. But often these are prayers about "stuff" and "things." I have heard people pray an entire prayer and never mention one person. Charles Haddon Spurgeon believed that the primary focus of prayer should be people. "Our prayers should include the concerns of those for whom Christ died".[3]

Jesus wants us to know that the authentic focus of prayer has to be people. Jesus did not come to die for buildings, although it's okay to pray for the building. He did not come to die for budgets, although it's okay to pray for the budget. Jesus came to die for people.

> For God so loved the world, [what God is talking about is not the entity of the world, but the people in the world] that he gave his only begotten Son, that whosoever believeth in him should not perish, but have everlasting life. (John 3:16, KJV)

God wants us to be concerned about people. Matthew 9:36 says that Jesus looked out on the multitude and had what? Compassion. That word means "God-like pity." It means not only to be sympathetic, but also empathetic. When you have compassion, you not only see someone in a situation needing help, but you go a step further and do something to alleviate the situation.

Our Lord said that if a person is hungry and naked, and you tell them to "be blessed" but you don't give them food and clothes, you have done nothing (James 2:15-16).

Jesus said, "When you come before Me, I am going to ask you some questions" (Matt. 16:43). The questions are going to be something like this:

- When I was in prison, did you visit me?

- When I was in the hospital, did you visit me?

- When I was hungry, did you feed me?

- When I was naked, did you clothe me?

- When I was thirsty, did you give me something to drink?

The disciples' response was (Matt. 25:44): "Lord, when did we see You hungry, naked, or in prison?" Jesus responded with what is called a "vicarious statement." He said, "As you did it to one of the least of these My brethren, you did it to Me" (Matt. 25:45). "Vicarious" means that what you do for one is applied to another. So whatever you do for the least, the lonely, the let-down, and the left-out, He says, "I am going to put it in My account and give you credit for it." Jesus, in verse 36, looks out, sees the multitude, and has compassion. Why? Because they were tired, weary, and scattered.

One Sunday, while I was on sabbatical, I went to a Tennessee Titans football game. Yes, I did! I had a good time, too! I saw people who came in short buses and had painted these buses with the colors of the Titans. My friend said we had to get out there at 8:00 AM. I said, "Our team does not start until 1:00 PM." He said, "You have to tailgate." I said, "Well, Lord," and I went to the game.

We arrived at the stadium at 8:00 AM and, to my surprise, the parking lot was already full! They had steaks, wine, and songs. I mean, they were having a good time. For four hours it was a party atmosphere. Then, for another three-and-a-half hours, we watched the game. Everybody was rooting—they were playing the Oakland Raiders (you know that's the only reason I went to the football game). We played the Raiders, and the Titans won. I noticed that even after the game, people went back to the parking lot and partied until nightfall. Then they went on their way.

I asked my friend, "Do you always do this?" He said, "We do this for eight home games." Now I did not ask him about this, but he said, "You know what? It's a strange thing. I see some of these guys on the street, and they don't even recognize me. These guys will not speak to or say anything to me. It's almost as if we're friends as long as we're in the stadium. When we get back into the real world, it does not matter." What I saw were seventy thousand people who were weary and scattered, as sheep without a shepherd.

Let me suggest to you that a lot of times the reason so many of us are going from one event or social gathering to another is because we really are weary and scattered. I have noticed that there are some people who cannot sit peacefully and quietly in their homes. They have to have two or three electronic things going on at one time because they really are weary and scattered, and they always have to have something on. I think that Jesus, if He saw us going about our daily activities, would have compassion. Jesus said we are "weary and scattered, like sheep having no shepherd" (Matt. 9:36, NKJV).

Then Jesus makes a statement. He says, "The harvest truly is plentiful, but the laborers are few" (Matt. 9:37, NKJV). This is not some sociologist making a statement. This is the Lord. He says, "Look at all these folks that are weary, scattered, and discombobulated, in a hurry, going nowhere." He says, "They are like scattered sheep. They are dressed for success, but they cannot take it when they get success. They want to be in a room full of people, but they are lonely when they are there. They are like scattered sheep."

Prayer Preserves Our Value in Ministry
Matthew 5:13–16

Why is prayer our focus? What do I mean by saying that prayer preserves our value in ministry? If we do not have an active prayer life, we will get caught up in religious activity and we will be going through the spiritual motions. In reality, we are not accomplishing anything. As Harvey Cox of Harvard University said, "If the Holy Spirit were to leave the local church and not show up again for twenty-five years, most churches would not even realize that the Holy Spirit was not there."

We have learned how to have church, to do church, and to be church without God. The San Francisco Giants would never try to play a game without a bat, ball, gloves, and some umpires. The San Francisco 49ers and the Oakland Raiders would never try to play an NFL game without a football. The San Jose Sharks would never play a hockey game without a hockey stick and a puck. The Golden State Warriors would never play a basketball game without a hoop, a ball, and some referees.

But it is amazing, amazing, amazing that we try to do church without God. The unfortunate thing is that we have become so good at having church without God, we do not really need the Lord! I am not talking about just my church. I am saying that there are millions who sit in church every Lord's day for two hours and really do not expect anything to happen. They are in church from 11:00 AM to about 12:30 PM. Let them out on time, and they are all right.

Jesus says, "When I see this crowd, I see weary and scattered multitudes, crowds like sheep without a shepherd." So brothers and sisters, you and I need to pray, because it preserves our value in ministry.

Matthew 5:13 says that you are the salt of the earth. "But if the salt loses its flavor [some translations read *loses its saltiness*], how shall it be seasoned? It is then good for nothing but to be thrown out and trampled underfoot by men."

Ladies—and some brothers who do cook—if you had a box of Morton salt in your cabinet, and you used salt to cook, but every time you used this particular salt, it just did not have any salty flavor, how long would you keep using that box of salt? Not long, right? Jesus is saying that when salt loses its ability to season, it has lost its reason for existence and it is then good for nothing but to be thrown out to the dung hill. In Jesus' time, people used it to patch holes in the sod.

Jesus also said:

> "You are the light of the world … [You do not] light a lamp and put it under a basket, but on a lamp stand … Let your light so shine before men, that they may see your good works and glorify your Father in heaven." (Matt. 5:14–16, NKJV)

We are *salt* and *light* to give *season* and *flavor* to this society; we are to give it *direction*. People are weary, wounded, and sad. When God places you where you live, labor, learn, or spend your leisure time, I will say it again: you are God on location. You are sent there. You are on a mission. You are an apostle, because "apostle" means "sent one." You are sent by God to where you are to let your light shine and to season, like salt. But Jesus says, "Listen, if you are not salt anymore, if you are not flavorful, then you are not giving direction, you are of no value, and you are good for nothing."

What is Jesus saying? When the saints have compromised their Christian witness, they are of no kingdom value. Prayer keeps us preserved so that we can do what God has called us to do. Prayer is *not* for God's benefit. Prayer is for *your* benefit.

When you pray, you are blessed. "Well, I have been praying, Pastor, and my prayers have not been answered. But, you know, I am praying more and more, and they are still not answered. I am still praying, but it is not answered."

The prayer is being answered because you are spending more time with God and, without even knowing it, you are becoming more in the image of Christ. You are looking more like Him. You may not even realize it is happening. But other people can see it.

Jesus said to His disciples, "The harvest truly is plentiful." Now, let us break that down. Jesus is saying that there are a lot of weary and scattered people in the world today, everywhere you look, no matter where you go. If you are in a room out in the community with ten other people, probably seven of them do not attend church anywhere. Jesus is saying, "Look out among you. Sinners." He is not saying "sinners" in a negative way. Jesus is saying, "People are out there who do not know Me. And the harvest is plentiful. Many people out there have ruptured relationships."

When Jesse Jackson came into the Bay Area at the height of the AIDS epidemic, he visited high schools and asked the high school students, "How many of you know at least one person who has died from AIDS? Or how many of you know someone who knows someone who has died from AIDS?" In the early years, there was just a handful. Now, when he comes to California, almost 80 percent of the audience stands up. They either know someone personally who has died from AIDS, or they know somebody who knows somebody who has died from AIDS.

Jesse Jackson continued by saying, "How many of you have been in a gang in Los Angeles?" Freshmen and sophomores are already in gangs. "How many of you know someone who has been killed by gang violence, is in jail for killing someone, or has been wounded? How many of you are in a gang?" In the early days, it was a small group; but now, most of the people know of someone who is involved in a gang.

The point Jesus is making is that there are a lot of people out there who are looking as if they have it all together. We spend billions of dollars a year trying to "fake it until we make it." We say, "If I don't feel good, at least I want to look good. If I don't have anything, I want to drive like I got something. If I am broke, you will never know it. I am going to fake it until I make it. I know I am spending more than I bring in, but I am just in-between blessings. God is going to turn it around."

We have a whole culture of people who are spending their lives trying to "image" their way through life. They are looking, masquerading, and perpetrating. Jesus says, "I look beyond the mask, and I see the misery. I look beyond the good looks, and I see the guilt. I look beyond the success, and I see the sorrow." Jesus says, "You are not going to fake Me out with how you look. You are not going to fake Me out with the talk. I have the 411. You are a sheep without a shepherd." And, Jesus says, the harvest is plentiful.

Prayer Places Us in the Provider's Presence (Romans 8:26)

Prayer not only preserves our value in ministry, as Matthew says, but prayer places us in the Provider's presence. Jesus says, "Therefore, pray." To whom? "The Lord of the harvest." He will send laborers. Now watch this! Jesus is really cool. Jesus is a genius. Listen to what Jesus says: "Everybody out there is looking like they have what they have not. What I want you to do is come to Me, and every time you see people like that, I want you to pray. I don't want you to be faked out by what they are driving, how good they look, how much money they have, or how they are dressed. I don't want you to be faked out. When they draw near to you—or when you get to know them—I want you to be in a posture of prayer. I want you to pray that God may give you an opportunity to minister. That is what I am looking for."

As you pray to the Lord of the harvest and you talk to Him, guess what you are doing? You must go into His presence, right? "Our Father, which art in heaven." You have got to make a connection.

Can I remind you about the Samaritan woman in John 4:7–29 who needed to meet Jesus? He sent the disciples into the town to buy meat. The woman came to draw water and Jesus said, "Give me a drink of water." He started a conversation. He had to send his disciples away so that He could have a one-on-one conversation with this woman because it was taboo for a Jewish man to talk with a Samaritan woman. Jesus said, "I have got to get you [His disciples] out of the way because you are so caught up in tradition that I cannot even do ministry in front of you. I have to send you away."

You may know someone who God has to get out of the picture so that He can do what He wants to do. He may send you on an errand so He can really get done what He wants to get done. "Why don't you take a thirty-minute break? Go have lunch and come back in. No, don't take thirty minutes—take an hour. Go take a long, extended lunch, and while you are gone, I can minister to someone." Sometimes God moves us aside in order to get His ministry done.

The more we are in God's presence, the more we want to be in God's presence. You do not say: "Well, you know, I don't go to the movies because I am trying to be spiritual. I don't go to the mall anymore. I am trying to be spiritual. I don't go here, I don't go there, because I am trying to be spiritual." That is the problem. You are *trying*. What we have to do is get to the point where we understand that it is more of Thee and less of me. We have to mature to the understanding that it is not where we are that makes us Christians—it's what's inside of us.

Jesus wants you to get in the habit. I have got to keep testifying; I have got to keep myself encouraged. My personal trainer keeps me working out, and I am seeing changes. At one of our staff meetings, our secretary had a wonderful Chinese lunch for us. She also had some chocolate Valentine cupcakes. Normally, I would get one for now and one for later. And, if they leave some in the refrigerator, I would get one when everyone left. But strangely enough, I had a good workout today and I had absolutely no desire to eat another cupcake. I am not saying that I am strong. But there is something about working out that diminishes my desire for sweets. When I am not working out, I want something sweet.

This same concept applies when we are in God's presence. The more we are in His presence, the less we want to do ungodly things. Not that we are trying to be better than anybody else; we just don't want to do those things anymore. It's changing us from the inside out. We are not "Holy Rollers." We are not "holier than thou." But there is something on the inside that's working on the outside. It is not a put-on. It is not a show. It is an inward desire to want to be like Jesus. Can anybody relate to that?

Look at Romans 8:26:

Likewise the Spirit also helps in our weaknesses. [Notice the word "weaknesses" is plural. Not just one. "I have got one thing I am working on." Well, there are some other things waiting in the wings. He says "weaknesses."] For we do not know what we should pray for as we ought, But the Spirit Himself makes intercession for us with groanings which cannot be uttered. (NKJV)

That is the reason why we have to get in God's presence—because then the Holy Spirit helps us.

The idea is that we become so caught up in our intimacy with God that things literally come out of our mouths that may not sound like English. But it is not speaking in tongues. It is an inner groaning that grows out of an intimacy that is legitimate. It is like being with God in such an intimate way that, to use a vernacular term, we "lose it." We lose it! We begin to praise God. We are not concerned about the audible; we are concerned about the internal. And that is a happy feeling, when you can just "let go and let God." You are not concerned about who is looking at you. You are not concerned about what time it is. You are not concerned about what the person leading the service is saying. You just get caught up. That is what happens most of the time in prayer. Have a little talk with Jesus!

Prayer Places the Premium on People
(John 3:16–19)

Let us turn to John 3:16. We may often read John 3:16, but, honestly, there are some verses after that that we also ought to read from time to time.

"For God so loved the world that He gave His only begotten Son, that whoever believes in Him should not perish but have everlasting [or eternal] life." (NKJV)

Look at verses 17 through 19:

"For God did not send His Son into the world to condemn the world, but that the world through Him might be saved.

"He who believes in Him is not condemned; but he who does not believe is condemned already, because he has not believed in the name of the only begotten Son of God. And this is the condemnation, that the light has come into the world, and men loved darkness rather than light, because their deeds were evil." (NKJV)

Jesus always has, and always will, love people. He came to earth to reach people. He died on Calvary for people. On the third day, He rose from the grave for people. Then, forty days later, He went back to glory. Now, the Bible says, He is at the right hand of God making intercession for people. Jesus says that one day He is going to come back and split the sky and come back for His people.

There will be no great cathedral in heaven, because the throne of God is all we are going to need. There will be no buses to ride on and no cars to drive, because there will be no need for them. He will be our "all in all." There will be no need for doctors, because there will be no sickness. There will be no need for lawyers, because there will be no cases to adjudicate. There will be no need for therapists and counselors, because everybody will be of one accord. The only thing that we are doing down here that we can transfer up there is the love that we show to people. We cannot carry anything else. Nothing else!

You have to start adding up your people value. How much time are you spending with people? We are becoming so depersonalized; so impersonal. Let me name some ways. We have a Social Security number. In the near future, you will be asked for your Social Security number before you are asked for your name, because once they have that number, they will know whether or not they want your name. We have PIN numbers—many of us have more than one PIN number. We have a password on the phone and on the computer. So depersonalized!

You have to make people pay attention to you as a person. You really have to do that. Sometimes I will go shopping and someone will say, "Can I help you?" and I do not say anything. They look up and repeat, "I said, can I help you?" And I say, "Oh, I didn't know you were talking to me. You were looking down."

When you are in class, you must make sure the teacher knows who you are. You must go up and introduce yourself. You may say, "I am not brownnosing." You should! Sometime you may have a test score of eighty-four, and a score of ninety is an A. Because the teacher knows you and likes you, what will he or she do? Give you six points. Let your teacher know you.

Application: Be Sensitive to People

I want to conclude with some things that I think are happening to us. Sometimes we say to people, "Why aren't you going outside the church and outside these walls; why aren't you witnessing?' As I was praying the other day, the Holy Spirit said to me, "Honestly, that is not where the people are." We do not have many who are willing to go out and knock on doors. That is not where the people are. So I want to respect that. The Lord said, "You need to start back at the basics and work your way up."

Application. The subject is prayer focus, and the focus is on what? People. I am going to give you some sensitizers—some things that will make a difference right now.

1. *Fellowship hour.* During fellowship hour at your church, make an intentional effort to go to someone you do not know.

Be intentional about going up to someone you do not know and say, "Hi, I'm Brenda. Welcome! Are you a new member?" And guess what? If you pray before you do it, then God might show you someone to go to who might have a spiritual need that you can meet. This is an example of one simple thing to help sensitize us during fellowship hour.

2. *Ministry meetings.* During your ministry meetings, do not just have a meeting: have an agenda, go through it, do a closing prayer, and go home. Sometimes, you might suspend all the business and just spend time saying to those at the meeting, "Hey, listen, is there anybody going through anything now? Are you struggling? Are there any prayer needs?" Sometimes the Lord might say, "Do not have a

business meeting; have a prayer meeting." The only way you are going to accomplish this is that you have to be sensitive. A lot of times—my church staff will tell you—I will come and say, "You know what? The Lord is saying we are going to pray today. We are just going to pray. No business. We will pray. That is going to be our business."

3. *Social gatherings.* We are a social people. At social gatherings, why not do ice-breakers and take time to sit down and make sure everybody meets everybody. Make sure that people leave the gathering knowing a little more about somebody than they knew before. There is no sense in us going across town to witness to somebody whom you are never going to see again, and yet you won't speak to the person in the pew right in front of you. First things first!

4. *The workplace.* Some of you have been working at the same place for thirty years, and right now, if your workplace took a survey and asked who the believers are, who are the saved, and who are the sanctified, your name might not even come up. Not because you are a bad person, but because you have never given any indication that you love the Lord. You did not offer one witness.

5. *School.* Lighting a light on a campus is a powerful thing. You do not have to act the fool in school. I have discovered that the kids in class who make the most noise are the ones who do not have their lesson done. Or, they left home hungry. Or, they are angry. They come to school to act the fool. That is the only reason they are coming. They have four Fs and two F-minuses, so they are not coming to study. They are the ones starting fights and all that. Why? Because they are either hungry, mad, upset, or being abused in so many kinds of ways. Young people: when you go to school, you need to let your light shine.

6. *Casual contacts.* You never know. One of our new members said that he was downtown and going through a difficult time in his life. His dad had just died. Someone came up to him and asked, "Do you go to church?" They did not read him the four spiritual laws; they just asked, "Do you go to church?" He said no. They invited him to church. That young man accepted Christ, and his life is changing dramatically. You do not have to know what the whole Bible says. You do not have to have it all together. Sometimes, a casual contact—somebody coming in to buy something—may leave going to heaven because of our witness.

Questions to Consider

1. *Does your prayer time focus on the needs of people?*

2. *Do you find yourself praying for things more than for people?*

3. *How does your focus on prayer need to change?*

6

The Prayer of Faith

Luke 18:1-8, Hebrews 11:6,
James 5:13-15

The *Prayer of Faith* is a kind of prayer that makes all the difference in the world.

This prayer seems simple on the outside, but it is deeper than what seems obvious. We are going to read James 5, in which James wrote that the *Prayer of Faith* will save the sick and will raise them up. It is a very powerful prayer. Hebrews 11:6 says that "without faith, it is impossible to please God, for he who comes to God must believe that He is, and that He is a rewarder of those who diligently seek Him" (NKJV).

Luke 18:1–8 gives us a portrait of the *Prayer of Faith*. Some of you have had to live it out without knowing what you were really doing. Once I tell you what it is, some of you will realize that you have already gone through situations that match the *Prayer of Faith*. If you look back over those situations that we are going to talk about and prayed your way through those situations, then you have experienced what the Bible calls the *Prayer of Faith*.

Luke 18:1: "And then He spoke a parable to them, that men always ought to pray and not lose heart" (NKJV). Now, often we miss great truths that are locked in one verse of Scripture. What the Lord is saying before He gives the parable is this: men and women ought never to faint or give out or lose energy, and the only way to avoid that is to pray. The only way you can keep on going through every situation is that you have to learn to pray about everything and in everything. Jesus is saying, "Here is what I want you to get: that you are always to pray and not give up." Then He tells us the parable.

In Luke 18:2, Jesus said, "There was in a certain city, a judge who did not care anything about God and nothing about humans" (paraphrased). Now, understand what He is saying. There was a judge who was a secular judge. He did not pretend to be religious. He had no desire to be religious, and not only did he not care about God, he really did not care about anyone else. He was self-sufficient. He had it all together; that was all that mattered to him.

This judge was faced with a widow (verse 3). This widow came to him, saying, "I have a case that really has merit against an adversary." The judge would not even listen to the case. But afterward he said to himself, "I do not care anything about God or anything about anybody else, yet this widow, by her persistence, is giving me fits. So I will listen to her case and I will argue favorably for her, lest by her continually coming, she just wears me out" (Luke 18:4–5, paraphrased).

Again, here is a judge who admits that he does not care anything about anybody. Spirituality is not his thing. But, here is a woman, a widow, who does not have any family or resources; yet, she wears him down with her persistence. He never admits it. He never lets the woman know it, but he says to himself in his chambers, "I do not care anything about this woman, but I am convinced that I am going to give out before she does. What I am going to do is rule favorably in her case."

> Then the Lord said, "Hear what the judge said. And shall God not avenge His own elect who cry out day and night to Him, though He bears long with them? I tell you that He will avenge them speedily. Nevertheless, when the Son of Man comes, will He really find faith on the earth?" (Luke 18:6–8, NKJV)

Here is what the Lord is asking: "If you are alive when I come back, will you still have faith?"

It says to me that there is the potential for me to give up on God so much so that there is nothing in my life that resembles faith. You see, the reason why we do not get faith is because we do not really understand how serious spiritual matters really are. We really believe that religion is a take-it-or-leave-it proposition. We believe that we have the right to be as involved with God as we choose to be. It is all up to us. We are not required. It is our call. We can choose what we want to do. If we do not want to do it, we do not have to. If we do not understand the seriousness of faith, then the possibility of not having it really exists.

For example, in the upper room, Jesus said to the twelve disciples seated with Him, "One of you twelve sitting around this table is going to betray me" (Mark 14:18). The Bible says in Mark 14:19 that everyone of them said, "Lord, am I the one?" What they were saying is that they understood what He meant. Although they walked with Him for three years, they had within themselves the possibility of backsliding. Some of you do not think you can backslide. You do not know that you can be in a backsliding state and come to church every Sunday. Backsliding has nothing to do with whether or not you come to church; it is whether or not God still has your heart as He once did. The Lord speaks this parable telling us not to lose heart.

Hebrews 11:6:

> But **without faith** it is impossible to please him: for he that cometh to God must believe that he is, and that he is a rewarder of them that diligently seek him.

Now, look at James 5:13–14:

> Is any among you afflicted? let him pray. Is any merry? let him sing psalms. Is any sick among you? let him call for the elders of the church; and let them pray over him, anointing him with oil in the name of the Lord:

Here is the subject, in verse 15:

> And the prayer of faith shall save the sick, and the Lord shall raise him up; and if he have committed sins, they shall be forgiven him.

What is this kind of prayer that is named the *Prayer of Faith*? This prayer is so powerful that it can literally bring back to life one who is apparently dead. This kind of prayer actually can cause people to repent and their sins be forgiven. This prayer has the ability to restore someone who has walked away from God. What type of prayer is called the *Prayer of Faith*?

There is something about the widow's prayer (Luke 18:3–5) that gives us an idea of what it is like. I have three examples of what it looks like:

1. Some of you have had to care for a child who may have been born with physical issues or for a child who has become seriously ill.

2. Some of you have had a spouse who has been ill to the point of death and recovered; some of you have had a spouse you have taken care of, and that spouse went on to be with the Lord.

3. Some of you have had to take care of parents who grew old and could not take care of themselves, and you had to minister to them. Your parents may still be alive, or they may have gone on.

We will now understand what the *Prayer of Faith* is and then we can look at examples.

Father's Love

The *Prayer of Faith* is a prayer that causes you to alter your entire life. When that loved one was ill, everything changed. As much as you loved that job, you had to say to those at work, "I have got to take a leave of absence," or "I am not going to be here every day." Right? Things changed. Your financial arrangements changed, because you had to divert money for daily expenses to care for this loved one. Your schedule changed. Your finances changed. Even your relationships changed.

One of the sisters in our church had to say to her husband, her children, and her grandchildren, "I love you all. I am committed to you, but my mom is seriously ill in Birmingham, and as much as I love you all, I am going to have to leave you. I do not know when I am going to come back, but it is my call to go to Birmingham and take care of her." It changed everything about her life for several months. The focus changed; the finances changed; schedules changed. When you understand how your life can be changed by a living arrangement, you understand what it means to pray the *Prayer of Faith*.

The *Prayer of Faith* shows you the Father's love. God loves us so much that He actually altered history to save us. He literally split the calendar between BC and AD to save us. The Father loves us so much that Jesus Christ, who was always with the Father from eternity, had to leave heaven and come to earth to save us. God altered eternity to save us. God changed the natural order to save us. God reconstructed history to save us. Whatever this *Prayer of Faith* is, it demonstrates the Father's love.

Focused

This prayer is focused. This prayer is done by passing everything else. When we pray the *Prayer of Faith*, we are saying, "I do not care what my favorite TV show is; I do not care what is on the sports channel; I do not care what sale is going on; it does not matter to me what is going on around me. I am going to be focused on this, and this alone." Everything else is excluded when one prays the *Prayer of Faith*. I want you to see that it is not something that you do one time and it's over. It is a focus of one's time and energy to God.

Fearless

Prayer becomes fearless. When you really decide to pray this prayer, the condition that you are praying about does not matter. You can pray about cancer and believe God will heal it. You can pray about domestic disputes and believe that God will heal them. You will become fearless in your prayer life, because you know that God always answers the *Prayer of Faith*. It is focused. It is fearless.

Faint-Proof

Prayer is faint-proof. In other words, you do not wonder *when* God is going to answer your prayer. You are confident that God *will* answer your prayer. Therefore, it is not the same as praying about the same thing over and over and over again. It is praying with the assurance that you are going to wear this problem out by continuing to lift it up to God. A lot of times we pray over and over and over about the same thing because we don't believe it's going to work out. We just keep mentioning it to God because we don't believe it's going to happen.

An example of that is when the saints were praying for Peter at the church in Mary's house. They prayed, "Oh, God. Peter is in prison. Oh, God. Release him, in the name of Jesus. God, You are able. God, You can. God, I know You will. You said we could ask anything in Your name, and You will do it. Oh, God. Hear our prayer tonight."

All of a sudden, there is a knocking at the door.

"Man, who is that bothering us when we are trying to pray? Oh, God. Send Your Spirit, send Your power, and send Your anointing. Come now."

More knocking at the door.

"Man, just when I get on my knees. Oh, God."

And on and on.

You see, those on the inside were praying a prayer of futility, but on the outside, Peter is knocking in faith (Acts 12:12-16).

This leads me to believe that a lot of our prayers are like those the early church was praying that evening. It is really praying in futility. Yes, we're saying all the right things and asking God all the right things. But deep down in our hearts, we really do not believe God is going to do anything. I know that you know that Brother So-and-So is ill, and Sister So-and-So is very ill, and we wonder when the service is going to be. All the time we're saying, "I am praying. But with that kind of cancer, you know, folks do not live. You know, they don't survive that." But we say, "Oh, I am praying for you. I believe in God with you." And all the time we're wondering what day of the week the memorial service is going to be. "Hope it isn't next Wednesday; that will alter my schedule."

The dangerous thing is that we can say all the right things, have all the right language about prayer, and seem sincere, yet, in our heart of hearts, we really don't believe anything is going to happen. As a matter of fact, we really believe that once we have prayed about it, we have done our job.

But to have the faith that believes it is going to happen we do not believe is our responsibility. In the example from Luke 18, this woman goes to the judge every day. "Judge, I have a good case. The case has merit. My enemy is wrong in this matter. And you know what? I am going to keep coming here. I just want you to know that. I do not care what day of the week it is or what time it is. I am going to keep coming until you hear my case, because my case has merit."

When you pray, do you have the sense that what you are asking God for really is a valid request? Does it have merit? "I am going to God about this because, honestly, this is something that I know God Himself is concerned about. I am going to keep going to God because I know the case has merit."

The widow said, "I am going to keep going to the judge because I know the case has merit. I know it does. It has merit. I am not whistling in the wind. This is a sincere case, God, and I am bringing it to You."

The human example is a woman who said, "Judge, I am just going to keep on coming, so you might as well get ready for me." She demonstrates it by continually coming. The judge says, "You know what? Better for me to go ahead and rule in her favor and give her exactly what she wants, because if I do not, she is going to [remember he is not spiritual] wear me out. I already know it. So, I will rule in her favor."

The power in this passage is this: a widow in the New Testament had no power. The judge did not have to worry about public opinion. She was a widow. She did not have anything going for her. If the judge had ignored her, nobody would have cared. She did not have any family, so there was no need for the judge to be concerned. But, even though she was powerless, she had something that was powerful, and that was persistence. Persistence! Just keep on coming. Keep on coming. Keep on coming. "I am going to do this."

That is the *Prayer of Faith*. If we were honest, many of us would not remember what we prayed for last week. We have no idea. "What did you pray about last Tuesday?" "I do not know. I would imagine I prayed, you know." Prayer becomes precious when it is important enough to write down what you are spending your time asking God for and bringing into His presence. Is it important for me to journal?

If I pray for my son to get a job, and I have prayed for nine months, and on September 13, 2004, he got the job, I want to journal that. Then the next time somebody asks me to pray for employment, I can go back and remember that when I prayed for my son, God answered my prayer. I have some ammunition in a past request being granted.

When I pray for you, I have one notch on my belt. Then, when God gives you your job, I have a second notch. Somebody says, "You know what? I have a promotion coming up, and it is serious. If I get this one, this is going to change my life. I am asking you to remember me in prayer because I know that you pray the *Prayer of Faith*." And you say, "What? I have two notches already. Let's take it on!" When that gets answered, you have three.

Let me make it plain. There is no sense in your telling people that you are going to be praying for their cancer when you have never prayed for someone to get a job. You do not have any notches! You have nothing! Now, cancer is one of the most serious diseases known to man, and someone tells you, "I have pancreatic cancer." Only 3 percent survive. You say, "I got this!" and you do not have any history of praying over tuberculosis, or the common cold, or anything like that. Come on! You have to have some successes in the small things of prayer to believe God for the greater things.

The truth is that most of us do not pray. It is not because we do not know how, but we do not have any success in it. We are not going to spend time doing anything that we are not good at. So start out praying for healing from the flu and the common cold, work your way up to heartburn, and then work your way up to ulcers. Then work your way up to tuberculosis; next, work your way up to cancer. Then raise the dead. Do not start out trying to raise someone from the dead. That is why it is important to journal, to write down what God has done in prayer.

Here are examples of what I am talking about and how prayer works:

Example 1. Upper room (Acts 2:1)—prayer. "When the day of Pentecost had fully come, they were all with one accord in one place" (NKJV). Remember, Jesus told them to do what? "Go to the upper room and wait until you are endued with power from on high" (Luke 24:49). The Bible says there were 120 of them—men, women, and children—in the upper room. The Bible indicates that they were praying. All with one accord, in one place, in one mind—praying. Then, ten days later, a miracle happened that fulfilled the prophecy of

Joel 2:28–32. The Spirit would be on everybody—men, women, and children. How did that happen? The saints were together in one place, of one mind, in one spirit, praying. A miracle happened because the saints came together and prayed the *Prayer of Faith.* "Jesus told us to come up here. Jesus told us to pray. We did it. Jesus did not say how long it was going to take."

If someone asks, "Now, what day are you going?" Some of us would say, "I will be there Monday." "When are you going?" "Well, I cannot go Monday; I will go Tuesday." "When are you going?" "I will be there this weekend." "When are you going?" "I will not be able to go there this time, but maybe next time."

When the Lord told the saints to return to Jerusalem, there were only a few members in the fellowship. When he instructed them to "Go and pray in the upper room," the number of disciples was 120. When Jesus told them to go and pray, guess how many went? 120. Do you see why there is no miracle in today's church? The reason is that you cannot get all of us to do anything. Why doesn't God move?

The saints went there in one accord, one mind, one place, and prayed for ten days. They didn't know how long it was going to take. They didn't worry about that. "We are going to pray because God said to go, and He is going to do something." Every member went.

I said this prayer is focused, right? The reason that we do not have the *Prayer of Faith* working in the church today is because it requires a majority of the members to participate in it. You see, one member doing this is not going to do anything. But with the majority of them coming together in one place, in one mind, with one accord, and with a "however-long-it-takes" and a "whatever-it-takes" attitude, miracles will break out everywhere.

You cannot tell me one activity that we could have in this church (or the church next door or the church down the street) that *every* member would come to. As much as we love our deacons, if one of them were to die, would every member be there at the funeral? You think so? No!

We love our church's "First Lady," don't we? But if Sister Van passed away, do you think every member would be there? No. There is no one in this church whose funeral, every member on the roster would come to—even with ten days' notice. I do not mean any harm, but Jesus could say, "I am going to be here in nine days," and I guarantee you, even if they heard the Lord Himself say it, some members would not be here. "Tell the Lord I will not be there, but if He leaves anything, save me some."

There is no activity that we can get all of us to do. Therefore, there are some blessings that we all will never get, because some things require everyone being in one accord, in one place, and of one mind in the Holy Spirit.

Example 2. Worship service (Acts 2:41–43)—prayer. Look at Acts 2:41–43. Now the church has grown from 120 to how many members? Three thousand! There were 120 in the upper room on the day of Pentecost. Now the church has grown to three thousand. Three thousand members were on the roll. Guess how many members showed up? Three thousand! It is in the text. Three thousand! Look at what happened! Talk about how prayer produces miracles. Verse 41 says that they all received the word *gladly*; verse 42 says that they continued in fellowship. Everybody is there. And the "fear" in verse 43—that is reverence. They are not frightened. They showed reverence for the "many wonders and signs [or miracles] [that] were done through the apostles" (Acts 2:43, NKJV). Three thousand members were all at the worship service. Peter brought an historical sermon that would have put all of us to sleep. He quoted from the Old Testament (Joel and Psalms) to show how prophesies were being fulfilled; we would not have made it. Then, as a result of that, signs and wonders were everywhere and were performed by just about all of the apostles. That is the *Prayer of Faith*.

What does the *Prayer of Faith* do? It gets everybody in the sanctuary. What does the *Prayer of Faith* do? It gets everyone fellowshipping with one another. What does the *Prayer of Faith* do? It gets everybody in the word. What does the *Prayer of Faith* do? It causes signs and wonders to break out in the congregation.

Example 3. Miracle of healing (Acts 3:1–9)—prayer. Peter and John were together, and they went to the temple to pray. Guess what time it was? Nine o'clock in the morning! It was not Sunday. It was 9:00 AM, and they were on their way to the first of three prayer services held *every* day. Some of you would not have made it. "I am a morning person. I guess I will be there." "I am a night person. You go on; I will catch you later." Sometimes God calls us to go against our natures and our natural tendencies so that we can receive a blessing.

The *Prayer of Faith* means that you pray when you don't even feel like it, but—what? It has become your custom. "No matter what, I am going to pray. I am not going to give up. I am not going to lose heart. I am not going to faint, because whatever happens, I am going to take it before the throne of grace. That is my custom."

Secondly, notice that on their way to the temple—to church—Peter and John encounter a man begging (verse 2). They stop long enough to minister. I lost you right there, because 99.9 percent of us would not stop for any reason on our way to church. We can witness a thirteen-car pile up—blood everywhere, arms and limbs on the freeway—and you know what we are going to do? Honk, honk, honk. We are going to weave our way through dead bodies to get to church. It will never dawn on us that maybe this is one of those Sundays when we need to forget about *going* to church and *be* the church.

Many of us have a lot of things to do that keep us from coming to church. But they are not Christ-centered things. I'm talking about baby showers and brunches and … you know. It has nothing to do with God, and we will not be there. But a thirteen-car pileup? Dead bodies, limbs, blood, crying? We are like the Indy 500 going on the high bank avoiding everything to get to church. Then, when we get to church, we come in and sit down and will not even wave our hands.

Peter and John go to church and, on their way to church, they see church in front of them and stop. The begging man expects to receive something. Peter said, "Silver and gold I do not have, but what I do have I give you: In the name of Jesus Christ of Nazareth, rise up and walk" (Acts 3:6, NKJV). They took the man, who had been lame since his mother's womb, by the right hand, picked him up, and the man started walking. Then, the man went to church with them.

Here is a man who is lame and who says, "Lord, I do not have any money." And you respond by saying, "I know what you want. I do not have what you want, but I have what you need. In the name of Jesus, get up!" You do not pray that kind of prayer unless you believe that God is able and you have seen God do it before.

On Sunday morning, there is a blind, crippled man outside in front of the church blocking the doorway so no one can get in. Everyone is going around him. They come in and say, "Isn't it a shame! On Sunday morning of all times! Here he is lying in front of the door. We cannot even get into the church house. We have to walk around and go in the side door because this man, who is blind and crippled and lame, is in front of the door." Not one of us, including the pastor, would ever think to go out there and stretch out a hand, saying, "I do not know what you want, but I know what you need. In Jesus' name, get up and come on in."

Every inconvenience is an opportunity to do that last thing: show compassion. Let me say it again. Every inconvenience is an opportunity to show compassion, and we miss it every day of our lives. Every inconvenience is an opportunity to show compassion, but you have to:

- Spend some time with God.

- Focus in prayer.

- Avoid distractions.

- Take and make the time to pray.

- Chart all prayer times in your schedule.

Also, it is very important that you spend enough time with God so that when you do come along and find that lame person, you already know how to handle it in the name of Jesus.

That is the *Prayer of Faith*. It will save the sick. It will raise the dead. It will work miracles. But it is done by persistent, customary, and undistracted time with God. No person, no thing, no one, and no situation gets in the way of your being with Him. God becomes your obsession. You do not have time for anything else but God.

I have a journal. This is what God is doing. I have a prayer list for the unsaved because God is going to save someone.

Prayer of Faith. Save the sick. Raise the dead. Forgive sin. Change lives. Alter destinies.

The widow woman did not have anything going for her, but she had something that the judge did not know anything about: prayer prayed persistently can change the world!

Questions to Consider

1. *What does faith mean to you?*

2. *How do faith and prayer work together?*

3. *How does faith affect physical healing?*

7

Keys to Answered
Prayer–Part 1

Luke 18:9–14

"He who humbles himself will be exalted" (Luke 18:14, NKJV). I want to begin with an insight concerning prayer that I had while talking to one of my relatives. This is a relative who was raised by her biological mother and father with no childhood trauma and no difficulties in the domestic arrangement. By and large, this relative had a blessed life. Her mother and father are still living. My relative can go as many as six months without talking to her father, who lives in the same vicinity—no great distance. She can go several months without so much as speaking to her father. My relative! This relative said that she honestly has no desire to visit. Again, she had no traumatic childhood experiences, but she can go for literally months without talking to her parents.

In my discussions with her, I said, "Well, tell me this: how is your prayer life?" The same family member said, "Well, honestly, I really do not pray very much." I caught a glimpse of this principle: if one has difficulty conversing with one's earthly parents, then one has almost no chance of communicating with one's heavenly Parent.

How we communicate with people on earth says an awful lot about how we communicate with our heavenly Father. In other words, if you do not communicate well with your brothers, your sisters, your relatives, or your friends at your job, then I can guarantee you that your prayer life is going to be null and void. There is not a lot of difference in how we talk to our earthly companions and how we talk to our heavenly Father. Think about that—literally going months without communicating!

If the truth were told, there are Christians who literally go months without authentic communication with God. I am convinced, saints, that prayer is not at the top of a lot of our agendas. We fail to see that communication with God should be our number-one priority. Not communicating with God results in our lives being in utter disarray. We are irritable. We cannot get along with anybody. Our relationships are torn and tattered because we do not communicate. I think that Jesus gives this parable in Luke to teach us how to communicate effectively.

Obviously, this parable tells us one thing: the Pharisee takes a whole lot of verses to say nothing. You must learn how to observe the cases when you are reading your Bible. Can I make an application right here? You can do a lot of talking and very little praying. Prayer does not consist of the amount of language used. Prayer consists of the intent of the heart of the pray-er. The Pharisee took a lot of time to say nothing, and the sinner took little time to say a lot. We need to get out of this notion, this myth, that our prayers have to be long and drawn out to be effective.

Nehemiah prayed one of the most powerful prayers of the Bible, and in essence he said, "Lord, help me" (Nehemiah 1:11).

Peter prayed one of the most effective prayers in the Bible when he said, "Lord, save me" (Matt. 14:30).

Stephen prayed one of the most compassionate prayers in the Bible when he said, "Lord, forgive them" (Acts 7:60).

Three words! "Forgive them, Lord." Three words! "Save me, Lord." Three words! "Help me, Lord." Why do we have to get a running start, take off on the runway, pray a long prayer, and then get up with no change in us or anybody else?

Standing Before God

The key to answered prayer is this: prayer is effective when we understand our standing before God. You are invited to pray because you *are*—not *going* to be—but *are now* the righteousness of God. You are positioned in perfect standing with God. There is nothing you have to do for God to hear your prayer. All you need for access to the throne of grace is to be a child of God. You do not have to be perfect. You do not have to have your life all together. That is a myth. You have to talk to God even when you are torn up and when you have blown it. You have to be encouraged to go to the throne of grace—so you are standing.

The reason you want to pray is because when God looks at us, He looks at us through the blood of Jesus Christ. You are forgiven. You are an heir. You are a child of the King. You are a Priest. You are in a right relationship with Him. You are standing.

1. *Religious person.* Notice the religious person. (You might call these the hindrances of prayer, or things that will hinder you from being heard.) First, this Pharisee in Luke 18 was caught up in himself. You have to be really careful, saints. You must be very careful that you do not mention yourself too much in your prayers. Do not call your name too much in your prayers. Do not get too personal in your prayers, i.e., "I," "my," "me," "mine," "us," and "we." When you get too much of you in your prayers, you may not be talking to God. You may be having a conversation with yourself.

The text says, "He was caught up in himself" (paraphrased). He says, "Now, Lord." He addresses God, but the Pharisee does not make contact with God. He directs his prayer towards heaven, but he never gets beyond himself. He compares himself to others. "I thank You." He had to be within earshot of the sinner. They are at the temple. He is talking to God and looking at the publican. "I thank You, Lord, that I am not like him." ("Thank God, that is not me.") He does not say, "If not for the grace of God, there go I." He says, "I thank You."

And the *words* he uses! This is what makes it so low-down. In the original manuscript, the Pharisees uses a Hebrew word that means "Allah," or "praise God." What the Pharisee is really doing is praising God for the fact that he is not like somebody else. He does not realize how far from God he really is.

"Lord, I thank You that I am not like her—don't dress like her, don't talk like her, don't look like her."

"I thank You, God, that I am not like him—don't dress like him, don't live like him, don't eat like him."

"I thank You that I have some education, so I thank You that I am not uneducated."

"I thank You, God, that I own property."

"God, I thank You that I am in the stock market. I sure thank You that I am not struggling like them."

"Lord, I thank You that I am not like them. Oh, how they smell so different."

This Pharisee is directing his conversation to himself. This is how your prayer can *not* be answered. "I am not like other men." In other words, "I am better."

This is one of those things that you and I, as Gardner Taylor said, would "never admit in polite company." The reason that many of us do not pray, and when we do pray, that our prayers are not heard, is that deep down in our hearts, we think we are better than other people. You are not going to admit that. If you admit that, maybe you are going to be changed, and you are not going to be changed.

But we have an arrogance about us as Christians that really makes God sick to His stomach. We do not realize how arrogant we are. We are ugly. We are snooty. And that smells like pride. We are not better off than anybody. There is absolutely nothing that we have today that cannot be taken from us. If it is not taken from us, there is nothing we have that we cannot leave.

Our health is one thing we cannot control. We can be sick this morning and in the funeral home before the sun goes down. We allow what we know, where we have been, what we have achieved, and what we have accumulated, to become so self-consuming and so self-absorbing that we are proud. And the sin is: we do not even know it. It would be one thing if this Pharisee were dead and buried. It would be one thing if the Pharisees did not have any living relatives among us. But the truth is that we are more pharisaical than we are willing to admit.

People may come to church not dressed as we think they ought to be dressed. This may be the first time they have ever been in church in their entire lives. Someone may have invited them. They may have been ready to give themselves to the Lord, but as soon as they come in, we look at them and make judgments. "Now where is she going? Look at her." And if somebody comes and smells a little bit like cigarettes or alcohol, or not as fresh as us, we think in our sanctified minds, "Let's ease on down the pew." We don't want to be next to him. All of these attitudes really do keep us from having answered prayer.

Look at this Pharisee. He was robed well. Pharisees were really the religious hierarchy of the day. They fasted twice a week. They tithed 10 percent of everything they had. They prayed three times a day. They went over land and sea to make a proselyte.

In Matthew 5:20, what did Jesus say? "Except your righteousness" does what? "Exceed." Pharisees are robed well. Pharisees are the intelligentsia of the day. Pharisees know the Torah and the Madras (a Jewish writing). Pharisees have the book; they know the law. They tithe on everything, even their investment property. Everything! Every week—at least two times, sometimes three times—they fast. Every week! They will go all across the country to get one disciple. So Jesus said, "… Except your righteousness shall exceed the righteousness of the scribes and Pharisees, ye shall in no case enter into the kingdom of heaven" (Matt. 5:20, KJV).

Jesus said, "I am going to give them their props" (paraphrased). Seemingly, the Pharisees had it all. On the outside, they were doing all the religious things that they were supposed to do. But Jesus said, "Except your righteousness exceeds theirs, you will not enter the kingdom." He is not saying that what they were doing was wrong. He is saying, "You ought to do as much or more than they do, but you ought to do it with"—what? The right attitude. You cannot say, "I do not tithe, but I am not a Pharisee." You cannot say, "I do not fast, but I am not a Pharisee." You cannot say, "I do not make a disciple over land and sea, but I am not a Pharisee." Jesus said, "Exceed them. Do what they do and more, but do it with the right spirit."

2. *Righteous person.* The Pharisee was not only a religious person, he was a righteous person. He praised God for what he was not. "I am not an extortionist." In other words, "I do not take advantage of others. I am not unjust. I do not commit sexual sins." He said, "They do their jobs." Some of us have not gotten by that yet—still tripped up over that. He said, "I do not do that."

Does it ever amaze you that sometimes sinners live better than saints? These sinners do not have any Holy Ghost, do not know any Bible, have never crossed the thresholds of a church, and many of them have been married sixty years and never committed adultery. Sixty years of marriage and never cheated on their spouses! No Bible; no Holy Ghost; no God; no prayer meeting; and no Bible study. And they live a good life.

Some of them will leave their entire fortune, perhaps millions of dollars, to charity. We, on the other hand, can be members of the church for 113 years and not leave the church a dime. "I love the Lord, He heard my cries / Heeded my every groan. / As long as I live, when troubles rise, / I'll hasten to His throne." However, we do not leave anything to the Lord. It never crossed our minds to put the church in our wills. We would rather leave our money to a son or daughter, knowing that our fortunes will be gone in six months.

Standing Before Men

"Look at them standing before me. I fast and I tithe." Saints, we have to be very careful that the good that we do in the name of the Lord is not being done for human consumption. We have to be very careful that our giving, our serving, and our living is not done so somebody can speak well of us.

I ask that you read 1 Corinthians 3 in your leisure time. Paul says that everything we do is going to be judged by fire (verse 12). If our work is considered wood, hay, or stubble, the fire will burn it up. Only that which you and I do with pure and sincere motives will give us a just reward.

For those of us who are not doing anything, you know you have nothing coming. When you get to heaven, you are going to be in the ghetto. It's one thing to live in a ghetto here, and another thing to live eternity in a ghetto. We amuse ourselves by saying, "All I want is just to have a seat somewhere. I do not have to be in a mansion. I would be satisfied with a tent as long as I am in the kingdom." It is not going to be very much fun for you to spend eternity looking at your brothers and sisters with fourteen-room mansions, and you are over in a ghetto. You'll have to go throughout all eternity bemoaning the fact, "I did not live by the law. I did not invite anyone to church. I did not visit anyone who was sick. I did not visit anybody in jail. I did not clothe them when they were naked. I did not encourage any downtrodden. All I did was within the church. I did my service." You will be in heaven, but you won't have a crown. Your head is going to be bald with no crown, and you'll be living in a pup tent. All the work that you did and thought you were getting paid for? The Lord will put a match to it, and 99.9 percent of it will be burned up.

We are talking about motives. The sad thing is that many of us are not doing anything. We say, "I am not doing anything for God." And other ones who are doing it are doing it for the wrong motives. We have to check ourselves. There are more of us in the Pharisee group then we want to admit—but it is true.

Standing Sinner

The sinner stands at a distance. Remember, Luke says that they both went to the temple. In the temple there was an inner court, then the outer court, and then the Gentile court. Everyone was not at the same place in the temple. This sinner stood in the outer court. He did not feel worthy to go anywhere near the Holy of Holies. He said, "You know, I am not even going up there. I do not deserve to go to the altar. I am going to be out there in the outer court because I do not even deserve to be that close to the altar. I do not deserve it. I am not worthy. I do not have anything to present myself to God. I have not anything that is spiritual. I am a sinner."

As a matter of fact, the idea of smiting the breast was self-flagellation. The idea was, "I know I am so unworthy—I hit myself to remind myself that I am not worthy." This is the opposite of the Pharisee's arrogance, "I thank You that I am not like him." It is self-mutilation. It is a self-bowing. "I am not worthy, so I am not even going to come to the altar. I am going to stand out here and not even look to heaven. I do not deserve that." Do you see him? "I am not going to look up. I do not deserve to even look towards heaven. To show that I am lowly, I am going to beat myself."

The sinner makes one request. In fact, any time that you and I go to God in prayer, there is really one thing that we need at that time. The sinner makes one request. He says, "Lord, I cannot look up. I cannot come near. I beat myself down. But I have one request: have mercy. If You just show me some mercy, that is all I need. I believe I can make it, Lord. Just give me some mercy."

Lamentations 3:23 says that He gives us new mercies every day. Imagine that all you need tomorrow morning is for God just to give you some mercy. The old folks say it like this, "Mercy suits my case. If I can just get some mercy, I could make it the rest of the way." Jesus, pointing to the sinner, said, "This man went down to his house made right, and the other did not." So prayer is not about us congratulating ourselves. Prayer is about exposing ourselves for what we need. Mercy!

Hebrews 7:25 says that the Lord ever lives to make intercession. I want us to get this. The Lord wants to hear from you. He really does. He wants you to make prayer a priority because you love Him. Prayer is not a catalogue of things that you need but just an opportunity to be in His presence. He wants to get us to the point where we just love communicating with Him. If He just gives us mercy, that is all we need.

This sinner gave us one of the shortest prayers in Scripture: "Lord, have mercy on me, a sinner." And that is all God needed to hear from him to make him right.

The sinner went home right. Check it out! But the saint went home the same.

The key to not getting your answer is pride. The key to answered prayer is humility.

Isaiah 57:15 is a good verse for us to look at. It says:

> For thus says the High and Lofty One
> Who inhabits eternity, whose name is Holy:
> "I dwell in the high and holy place,
> With him who has a contrite and humble spirit,
> To revive the spirit of the humble,
> And to revive the heart of the contrite ones." (NKJV)

Therefore, when you go to God contrite and humble, God makes intercession for you to meet your need, even when you don't know what to pray for.

Romans 8:26 says, "For we know not what we should pray for as we ought: but the Spirit itself maketh intercession for us with groanings which cannot be uttered" (KJV). When the man said, "Lord, have mercy on me, a sinner," the Holy Spirit, in turn, said, "All right, Lord, he asked for mercy. What he needs is a blessing."

All you need to do is ask God for one thing. Say, "Lord, let me just be content with being in Your presence. For in Your presence is joy evermore. In Your presence is strength. In Your presence is wisdom, understanding, and knowledge."

When you pray and ask for what you really need, the Holy Ghost will interpret some wants and add that to your prayer. Humility is not judging others, but being humble and saying to God, "I do not have anything You would want from me." We do not have anything.

I hate to burst your bubble, but I heard Jesus say, "Without Me, you are nothing" (John 15:5). I know you have been taking courses in self-esteem. I know you have been taking courses on how to think highly of yourself. I know you have been doing your daily affirmations and reading your daily word and speaking over your life.

But I have to tell you something: without God, you are nothing. Nothing! You can affirm all day long, but you are still nothing. It is Him. It is in Him that we "live, and move, and have our being" (Acts 17:28, KJV).

Questions to Consider

1. *How would you define humility?*

2. *Can humility and confidence work together?*

3. *Do you allow your personal failures to hinder or block intimacy with God?*

8

Keys to Answered Prayer–Part 2

I Peter 5:7

1 Peter 5:5–7 reads:

> Likewise, ye younger, submit yourselves unto the elder.
> Yea, all of you be subject one to another, and be clothed with
> humility: for God resisteth the proud, and giveth grace to the
> humble.
> Humble yourselves therefore under the mighty hand of
> God, that he may exalt you in due time:
> Casting all your care upon him; for he careth for you.
> (KJV)

In my opinion, when Adam and Eve were created, they had
unlimited intellectual power, unlimited physical strength, and
unlimited spiritual capacity. In reality, they were geniuses, unlimited
in all capacities. After their fall, and consequently for all of us, humans
still retained the image of God within.

But the truth is, we are all fallen creatures. None of us lives up to
the inner capacity—intellectually, physically, or spiritually—that we
possess. We still have the image of God, but we do not use all of our
abilities. It has been said that even the brightest among us use less than
10 percent of their brainpower. Consequently, we only have a limited
capacity spiritually, physically, and intellectually. Therefore, we have to
decide what we are going to put in the hard drive of our minds.

Remember, capacity is limited, so we have to commit to what we
are going to expose our minds to, what we are going to expose our
hearts to, and what we are going to expose our spirits to. We have to

commit ourselves to something, and therein lies whether or not we grow.

Pride is the opposite of humility. The reason that we cannot contact God as we would like to is that we are more full of ourselves than we are full of God. Remember: limited capacity. You cannot be full of self and full of God. You have to determine which one will be preeminent in your life—which one will be your priority in your life. "Am I going to be filled with God's spirit, or am I going to be filled with my flesh?" You can't have both. You have to decide.

The result of pride is always anxiety. When you and I commit ourselves to handling our own lives, the result will always be anxiety. You cannot trust in yourself and trust in God. You have to determine in whom you will trust. "Myself and my abilities, or God and His supernatural abilities?"

Revisit Humility

Previously, we talked about the arrogance of the Pharisees on the subject of prayer and the publican. The publican would not even lift up his eyes toward heaven; he just said, "Lord, have mercy on me, a sinner" (Luke 18:13). We have to revisit humility. We have to understand that God humbles the arrogant, but He gives grace to the humble.

No one actually thinks that he or she is proud. If you asked anyone if he or she were humble, the person would probably say something like, "Yeah. I'm not proud. I thank God for my achievements, my accomplishments, and my accumulations. I thank God for it, but, you know, I'm not proud. I'm humble. I don't think more of myself than I ought to. Yes, I am gifted. I possess more than others. But I'm not proud. I give God credit." The truth is, when you say you are humble, you're proud, and when you say you are proud, you're proud.

Let us talk about keys to answered prayer. How are we assured that we are heard from on high? 1 Peter 5:5–7 begins by saying that right relationships in the body will be foundational to our prayers being answered in heaven. It seems to be a simple matter, but it is one that the saints often neglect and overlook. You cannot be at odds with your brothers and sisters and be in a right relationship with God. We act any kind of way; treat people any kind of way; do what we want to do;

and then we bow our knees to God as if our behavior and our beliefs are not bound together.

Jesus taught that if you bring a gift to the altar and then remember that you have fault against someone, leave your gift at the altar. Go and be reconciled to your brother or sister, and then come back and offer your gift (Matt. 5:24). The Lord is saying that if there is ill will between you and your brother or sister, your gift does not register in heaven's economy. Even your giving is contaminated if your relationships are not right. Many of us just go on with business as usual and we think our relationship with God is all right, even though we mistreat others knowingly and intentionally.

You may say, "Well, I can bypass that and go right to God. I do not need anyone. You know, I am my own priest. I do not need anyone to make mediation for me. I can go to God for myself. It does not matter how you think or what you think. I don't need you. I can go right to God." What you are really doing is closing the door to answered prayer.

Key #1—Right Relationships Within the Body

1. *Respect elders chronologically.* Respect your elders—both your chronological elders and your spiritual elders. Peter said in verse 5 that in the body of Christ (the Christian community), those who are chronologically older than you are due respect. It is very simple. Children do not call grown people by their first names. Imagine a three-year-old saying, "Hey, Larry, what's up?" "How you doing, D. C.?" "Hey, Dennis. How you doing?" Unfortunately, the parents do not correct them. That is not cute. They are not cute. The chronological elder is to be respected. And, when you do not respect your elders, the text tells us that it hinders your prayers.

We live in an age now where young people think, "Old folks have nothing to say. They can't tell me anything. I've been there before. I know what I am doing. I do not need any advice." But verse 5 says that the younger are to *submit*. Younger people are to bow down to their elders out of respect. That is a sign of humility. The elders were here before you were. They know more than you do. Even if they do not know more than you, treat them like they do. Respect them!

2. *Respect elders spiritually.* Hebrews 13:7 says to honor those who rule over you in the Lord. God set it up so that there are those who rule spiritually over you. You cannot be a Lone Ranger Christian. You cannot decide who you are going to honor and who you are going to obey. Honor those who have rule over you—elders. When you desecrate a man of God or a woman of God, you do damage to your soul. Arrogance and pride is what hinders your prayers.

3. *Respect one another.* Verse 5 continues, "All of you be subject [or bow yourselves] one to another" (KJV). "Out-loving" one another is an idea that you and I ought to try. "How much love can I show you? How much can you show me? How much love can we show one another?" Christianity is love in action. You cannot love God, whom you have never seen, and hate your brother and sister, whom you see every day. You cannot bypass people and get to God. You have to get to God through people. That is the key.

Think about it. Is there anyone against whom you have animosity or an ill spirit? Matthew 18 says that you are supposed to reconcile that. Go to that person one-on-one and try to talk it out and pray it out. If the person won't listen, go get two or three other saints, and try again. If the person still won't listen, bring the person before the church. 1 Corinthians 5:5 goes on to say, "To deliver such a one unto Satan for the destruction of the flesh, that the spirit may be saved in the day of the Lord Jesus."

In the body of Christ, the inability to get along with others is a serious issue. When you break fellowship, you break the power line between heaven and earth. That is how serious it is. God works through us, and we must be of one accord.

Key #2—Right Relationship With God

In my travels attending conferences and workshops, I have come to the conclusion that the body of Christ does not practice Scriptural principles. We worry more than we pray. We are more concerned about ourselves than we are about anybody else. I see this in my own family. If I give my family members a choice between building up and tearing down, they choose to tear down every time. Is your family like that? This tells me that if biological brothers and sisters beat up on one another, then you should not be too surprised when believers do the same thing. When you cross that threshold, nothing spiritual will happen to you.

If you are a devil on Devil's Mountain, you are going to be a devil on the ground.

1. *Mighty hand means respect His power—not doubting.* In talking to someone the other day, we discussed a friend of ours who was diagnosed with pancreatic cancer. This someone prayed, and here is what he said: "Lord, we know You are able to heal pancreatic cancer, because You can do anything but fail. We know You have the power. Touch now, in Jesus' name. Amen." As soon as he had finished praying, do you know what he said? "You know, pancreatic cancer—you don't always survive that. That is the number-one killer." Then he said, "The actor Patrick Swayze has pancreatic cancer. He's a goner."

We have the capacity to pray for something in one voice and, before the words cool off, we speak doubt for the one we just prayed for. "God, I know that You can bless the economy, and no matter what is going on out there, I know You can still make a way." "Lord, I do not know how I am going to pay my mortgage. I have a subprime loan here. Lord, have mercy—hmm, hmm." Do you see? Doubt and faith cannot coexist.

We have a limited capacity. We cannot fill our minds with junk from television, radio, and the Internet. We cannot set our hearts to crave the things of this world or allow our spirits to be contaminated by materialism and selfishness and still think our prayers can be heard. 1 Peter 5:6 says that you have to humble yourself under the mighty hand of God. You have to bow to the sovereignty of God. If you do not humble yourself, it is impossible to grow.

When I was teaching Spiritual Formation at Golden Gate Baptist Theological Seminary in Mill Valley, California, I asked the students to keep a two-week log of every waking hour, from the time they awakened until the time they went to bed.

You should, as an experiment, try logging your time for two weeks. Keep up with every waking moment. These moments include the hours that you are on your job and the hours when you are at home. Pay close attention to the amount of time you spend watching television and talking on the telephone, and to whom you associate with. After two weeks, I guarantee that you will be able to tell that you have grown stronger or, if you are weak, you will able to understand why you are weak.

It is what we do with our time. We watch junk on television from the time we get off work or the time we get out of school until the time we go to bed, and then we watch the evening news in bed. In the morning, we get up, turn the television on, and listen to it again. While on the job, we talk about how bad things are. Our minds are full of garbage from consuming the garbage on television.

2. *Trust God with the timing of your exaltation or answered prayer.* God wants to bless you more than you want to be blessed. The one who is primarily responsible for blocking your blessings is you. It is a liberating thing but also a responsibility when you understand that the only one who can keep you down is you.

When you realize that you no longer have someone else to blame for your situation, and no one else can take the rap for who you are—or who you are not—then you can assume the awesome responsibility of saying, "I have to live responsibly every moment of every hour, every hour of every day, every day of every week, every week of every month, and every month of every year."

Your attitude should be: "How high I go is up to me. How low I stay is up to me. How wide I become is up to me. How spiritually I have grown is up to me. No one besides me can be the most loving, the most kind, the most considerate, and the most humble human being that ever walked the face of the earth. No one can out-love me. No one can beat me at being nice. No one can be more positive than I am. As a matter of fact, I am going to win the marathon of being the nicest person in my home and the nicest person on my job. I am running to be the nicest in my church. That is my goal. I am going to be syrupy sweet. I am going to be generous. I am going to be understanding. I am going to be considerate with my time. I am going to be so loving that the angels are going to be hating on me."

Nobody but you can keep you from being all that God wants you to be. Stop giving your power away to somebody else. Stop playing the blame game. Only you can seek God's blessings for you, and only you can stop yourself from being blessed.

3. *God cares for you and your situation.* We doubt that God cares for us because we do not take our burdens to the Lord and leave them

there. Valium and Xanax are not just being purchased by sinners. The saints have antidepressants in their purses and in their pockets. They say, "I am praying." Actually, you are praying and popping. I'm sure we all know someone who is on prescription medication for nerves. Saints who are on medication are those who refuse to take their burdens to the Lord and leave them there. Of course, there are some who need medication. There is a reality in being bipolar or having some other mental health problem. But there is no excuse for saints to use Valium or Xanax. Those are saints who are living stressful lives but have not given their lives and their stress over to God.

Key #3—Turn It All Over to Him

Peter says to cast your cares upon Him. Turn it over to Him. Psalm 121:3–4 says that God does not sleep or slumber. Do you know what this passage is trying to tell you? Why are you staying up all night when God is going to be up anyway? Just give it to God and go to sleep. "Cast" means to throw it on God.

When the phone rings at my house, the first thing I do before I answer the phone is pray, "Lord, give me wisdom. And for whomever is calling, give me the right words to say." It is that serious. I get a lot of bad news on the phone from different parts of the country and sometimes different parts of the world. I do not answer the phone until I spend time with God.

1. "*Cast" means to throw it onto God.* Have you ever gotten busy and just took off right away doing things and then realized mid-morning that you did not spend time with God? Then things start bombarding you and you cannot do anything right. You say, "Okay. I know what it is. I have to back up and get with God."

Before you begin to worry about it, throw it to God and say, "Here it is, Lord." Don't try to carry it; give it to God. Tell God, "Lord, I cannot handle this, and even if I thought I could, I don't want to because You can handle it better than I can. Take it, God." Just throw it on Him. That is what the writer in 1 Peter 5:7 is saying. Cast your cares, or throw your cares, on God. Why? Because God cares. God does not want you to handle the things that you think you can handle, and then give Him the things you think you can't handle. You can't handle any of it. Give it all to God. If you think you can handle some of the things, you are just fooling yourself. You can't handle them. Just give them *all* to God. Cast your cares on Him, for He cares. Throw it to Him, and throw it to Him first. I repeat: throw it to Him first! Kerwin Lee states, "When a situation arises that tempts you to worry, you have to get rid of it quickly. Get it off you. God desires that we give him everything that you are worried about."[4]

How many of you ladies, before you would do anything when something came up, would call your mom and talk to her about it? And, guys, if you had a father figure and something came up, how many of you would call Dad and ask, "Do you know anything about this?"

2. *Throw it to Him first and quickly.* Most of us do not take these situations to God first. We say, "How am I going to handle this?" We go to work, and before we know it, we are trying to solve it. If we are fortunate enough and have enough of whatever it takes to solve it, we never bring God in on it. We cannot give God praise. Why? Because *we* did it, and we don't even try to give Him praise after we've done it. We say, "I want to thank You for helping me to get through it," when we know we have done it ourselves. God does not want false or phony praise.

3. *He cares.* "Cast" means that I throw it onto Him first, and quickly, because He cares. When I was growing up, there was a song we sang in our church titled "God Cares." The lyrics were: "In a mansion made of stone / or in a shanty all alone, / God cares. God cares. / He cares for you." No matter your gender, no matter your age, no matter your race, no matter your circumstances, God cares. He is not going to allow us to be overwhelmed or overcome by the situations that we encounter.

Can I stop and caution us that we cannot ask God to bless a mess? Sometimes the saints want to go against the revealed will of God, the word of God, and good common sense. Then, after we go against the will and word of God, we want God to bless it. I believe that this is the reason why 80 percent of the saints fail in our problems. We are doing things in our own mind, and we want God to bless that.

Do not ask God to bless a relationship after you have gotten into it and fornicated or engaged in all kinds of sexual sin. Then you realize that you are in love and say, "God, bless it. Hold us together, Lord." When it doesn't work out, you say, "God, You helped Daniel get out of the lion's den. I know You can fix this!" The truth is that you should never have gone there.

Saints ought to be wise enough to go to another saint and say, "I am thinking about getting involved in this relationship, and I know you are a man/woman of God. What do you think?" Or, "I know you are in the word of God. Pray with me about this decision." Or, "I know that you have walked with the Lord a long time, and I think I am in love. Would you come and talk with me, pray with me, and give me some advice about this?" "I feel like something is going on, and I love him, but I don't want to go too far. I want to sit down with the elders."

Unfortunately, today's Christians say, "It's no one's business who I date or sleep with, or what I do. It is no one's business. Nobody can tell me what to do. They are not perfect. If I make a mistake, let me live with it. You made your mistakes. No, I will not talk with the saints."

Key #4—Watch the Devil

1 Peter 5:8 says, "Be sober, be vigilant; because your adversary the devil, as a roaring lion, walketh about, seeking whom he may devour" (KJV).

1. *The Devil is loudest when our need is greatest.* Remember this: the devil roars loudest when your need is greatest. When you are really up against that which you know is beyond your capacity to handle—a financial crisis, medical diagnosis, family need, a child in some relationship—that's when Satan shows up roaring, "Where is God now? Where are the saints now? You are all by yourself. Nobody cares about you. Look at you. Why not quit church? Quit God? Where is God now?"

I admit that sometimes God does seems slow to respond. Sometimes we wonder why God does not show up by shooting Satan or cutting him up. Sometimes we want God to kick down the door. We may say, "Come on, God. Why didn't you tell me I had a tumor?" Then the devil shows up again to point his finger and ask, "Where is God now? Where is God now? Where is God now? Look at all you have done for God. Where is God now?" The devil is loudest when our need is greatest.

But, instead of us giving a hand to our brothers and sisters, we'd rather give a hand to the devil.

2. *Do not get drunk on your issue.* 1 Peter 5:8 says to be sober. God does not want anyone getting drunk on the issue or problem. Do you know people who have gotten drunk on their issues? They seem to turn their problems over and over and over and over and over. Being sober means do not get drunk. Have you ever done that?

"Man, The doctor said so and so. Oh my, oh my." You are depressed.

"Oh, I have breast cancer. I wonder if it is malignant. What if they take my breast? Will he really love me anymore? How long will I live? Probably going to die. Oh, God." You are getting drunk on the issue.

"My child is smoking pot. Oh, God. Next will be heroine, then cocaine. He is going to get a needle, then he is going to get AIDS … then he is going to die. Oh, God."

"Found a birth control pill in my daughter's purse. Oh, God. HIV is next. Oh, God." Do not get drunk on the issues.

Money might be short now, but that does not mean money is going to be short always. We may just be in between lessons. You will never get to the mountain without first going through the valley. Where you are now is not where you are going to stay. You might be just passing through. So, don't get drunk on the issues. Do not keep mulling them over and over and over and over and over. "What if? What if? What if? What if?" I've heard it said that most of the things we worry about never happen.

3. *Keep watch.* Do not allow your blessings to lift you so high that the air gets rare and you stop watching. Do not allow your issues to bring you so low that you stop trusting. Keep watching. Keep watching. Keep your eyes on the prize of the Lord.

4. *Anxiety is unnecessary.* Cast your cares upon Him. Do not worry. Do not get caught up. Do not get drunk on the issues, because anxiety and worry are unnecessary. No one ever grew an inch taller by worrying. Worry is a friend only to the undertaker. The only thing that worry is good for is getting you to the grave more quickly than you would normally have gotten there. "Long-term exposure to stress can lead to serious health problems. Chronic stress disrupts nearly every system in your body. It can raise blood pressure, suppress the immune system,

increase the risk of heart attack and stroke, contribute to infertility, and speed up the aging process. Long-term stress can even rewire the brain, leaving you more vulnerable to anxiety and depression" (Helpguide. org). You can literally worry yourself to death. It is not necessary.

5. *Anxiety is unprofitable.* What will it profit a man or a woman to gain the whole world and lose his or her soul (Mark 8:36)? What would you give in exchange for your soul? Worry is unprofitable. The Dow Jones of Worry never goes up—it always goes down.

6. *Anxiety is unbecoming.* When praising God, some of us may shout, faint, speak in tongues, and roll on the floor. However, when something hits you hard, you quit church. That is unbecoming. Also, walking around looking like you have lost your best friend is not becoming. "What is wrong with you?" "How would you know? If it's not one thing, it's another. It's hard." Just last week, you were dancing in the church. Now, because you are worried, you have become joyless.

Questions to Consider

1. What things do you worry most about?

2. What things do you pray most about?

3. After prayer, does worry decrease, increase, or remain the same?

9

Keys to Answered Prayer–Part 3

John 6:1–13

We are still looking at the question, "How do we get answered prayers?" How can we have our prayers answered? We want God to hear and answer our prayers now. John 6:1–13 is a familiar passage, but I want us to look at this story with new eyes:

> After these things Jesus went over the Sea of Galilee, which is the Sea of Tiberias. Then a great multitude followed Him because they saw His signs [His miracles] which He performed on those who were diseased. And Jesus went up on the mountain, and there He sat with His disciples.
>
> Now the Passover, a feast of the Jews, was near. Then Jesus lifted up His eyes, and seeing a great multitude coming toward Him, He said to Philip, "Where shall we buy bread, that these may eat?" [The key to understanding this is in the next verse.] But this He said to test him, for He Himself knew what He would do. [Remember, whatever happens, the Lord had already decided what He was going to do.]
>
> Philip answered Him, "Two hundred denarii worth of bread is not sufficient for them, that every one of them may have a little." [Now mark that.]
>
> One of His disciples, Andrew, Simon Peter's brother, said to Him, "There is a lad here who has five barley loaves and two small fish, but what are they among so many?" [Watch the context.]
>
> Then Jesus said, "Make the people sit down." Now there was much grass in the place. So the men sat down, in number about five thousand. And Jesus took the loaves, and when He

had given thanks [There is the key. That is prayer, right?] He distributed them to the disciples, and the disciples to those sitting down; and likewise of the fish, as much as they wanted. [Remember "little," "want."] So when they were filled, He said to His disciples, "Gather up the fragments that remain, so that nothing is lost." Therefore they gathered them up, and filled twelve baskets with the fragments of the five barley loaves which were left over by those who had eaten (NKJV).

Keys to Answered Prayer
John 6:1–13

Whenever we begin to look at life through the same old eyes, we begin to become diseased—and that leads to decay, and then death. God really wants us to learn to look at every situation—every day—with brand-new eyes. In other words, the way you looked at things yesterday and the way you will look at things tomorrow has to be different. He does not want us to always look at life through the same lenses.

If we continuously look at life the same way, we become "stuck." We become locked-in. We become traditional. We become so static that growth does not take place. The challenge is that even though you live life much the same way, try to look at life differently.

We may ask, "How do I look at life differently when I work at the same location where I worked last year? How do I face my employment differently?"

"I am married to the same woman."

"I am married to the same man."

"I have the same friend that I have had for years. How do I look at this relationship differently?"

"I go to the same church that I have been going to for years."

"How do I not allow the sameness of my life to lock me down? How do I learn, in Christ, to see new possibilities every day?"

That is the challenge!

If we were to be honest with ourselves, I assure you that most of us are living life in a rut. We eat the same things most of the time. We wear the same clothes—we have a closetful, but we have been wearing the same thing over and over again. We have four or five different ways we could go, but we go in the same direction all the time. We talk to the same people every day—call Mom in the morning, sister in the afternoon, and best friend at night. Life is one real recipe for blandness.

Even when it comes to God, our expectations of God are so bland and limited and vanilla that we do not ask anything different of God. We do not believe anything different from God. Our lives, for the most part, are the same because we are looking at life through the same eyes. Most of our eyes are not alive, but dead. I believe that God is trying to challenge us as His people, individually and collectively, to see life in brand-new colors every day so that we will not allow the sameness of life to lock us down.

I have discovered that if we are not careful, the same thing will happen when we study the word of God. We look at stories. We see the same characters. We interpret them the same way. We have the same beginning of the story. We have the same conclusion. We don't see anything different because we're looking at the story with the same eyes.

I believe God is saying, "Don't ever allow sameness to invade your spiritual life so that you get the same thing all the time." As a matter of fact, as a child of God, life is supposed to be a series of valleys and mountains; shouts and silences of praise; normal days and extraordinary days; and sometimes miracles. It is totally different. We ought not to want our life to be the same. The kids have a word for that: boring! Saints, we cannot allow boredom to invade our spiritual lives, our faith, and our relationships. Then there is nothing new—nothing ventured, nothing gained—because everything is the same.

Now, let us look at the story. Jesus returns to the crowd after having worshipped. He sees a throng of people coming to Him. He asks a question. He says, "What are all of these people going to eat?" When we put the gospels together—Matthew, Mark, Luke, and John—one gospel says the crowd had been out there for three long days having church. They were so excited in God that they forgot to eat! I know you cannot identify with that! But they did. Three days! After they were caught up in the spiritual transformation, they realized, "We have not eaten in three days!" Jesus says, "What are we going to feed them?" That is where our text comes. What were they going to do?

I want you to look at what the disciples said, and then I am going to give you something new and different. First of all, Philip says in verse 7, "We have two hundred denarii worth of bread, but what is that among so many?" Now, let us do some math—five thousand men, not counting women and children. The average family in Palestine during this time had two to three children. We count five thousand men, and if they were married, we are talking about at least twenty thousand hungry people. Philip says, "We have two hundred denarii worth of money in the treasury." A denarii was one day's wages. They have about two hundred day's wages, or about seven months' worth of money, in the treasury. The disciples look at the money and the size of the crowd, and they conclude that that would not be enough for everyone to get a little piece of something to eat.

Attitude Concerning What We Possess

The number-one reason that many of our prayers are not answered is our attitude concerning what we already possess. Most of us cannot receive the miracles that God has for us because we are truly hung up on what we already possess. Little or much—it is just attitude. "A bird in the hand is worth two in the bush." "I don't have enough to do what I need done, but I'm going to hold on tightly to this little bit that I have." We hold on so tight that nothing can get in, nothing can get out—so, nothing goes out, and nothing comes in. T.D. Jakes asks, "What do you want to be about? What is your vision, your purpose, and your mission? When we grow into ourselves, learning from our mistakes we become content with who we are."[5]

The kingdom economy is this: the generous soul is made fat. When you allow God to freely control what comes in and what goes out, then God takes on the responsibility of making sure that you always have enough. But when you say, "I've got a little, and I've got to manage it," God says, "Okay. I will let you manage it." When we manage lack, it becomes greater lack.

The number-one thing that keeps us from really entering into what God asks for us is our attitude toward what we already possess. I am not just talking about money. You cannot become content with all that you know right now. If you do not increase your accumulation of knowledge—of good information—what you know now is not going to be adequate next year. You have to constantly bring in more information, more knowledge, more experience.

If you keep hanging around the same people, you are only going to get from them what they already have. If you do not enlarge your circle of influence or if you do not bring around you those who can challenge you, then you are not going to grow. If you stay where you are now, you're going to be behind next year. So you honestly need to change your associates, because all they want to do is enough to get by. And you, without knowing it, have developed the same attitude. You are no longer trying to strive because you are around people who are comfortable, and you have become comfortable. God's desire is to comfort the afflicted and afflict the comfortable.

In verse 8, one of the disciples, Andrew, the brother of Simon Peter, said, "There is a lad." Here is where the revelation comes in. Watch the context, and you will see what this story is really all about. They have two hundred days' worth of wages, but that's not enough, right? In the same context, they say, "But there is a boy who has five barley loaves [that's the size of a really, really, really large bagel] and two small fish."

So, this boy has five large barley loaves and two fish. The revelation is that this boy is not just any boy. I believe that he is really a boy who has set up a concession stand. Five barley loaves are too much for one person to eat. This was not the boy's lunch. It was some loaves and some fish that his mom probably gave to him and said, "There is a crowd of several thousand over on the grass. This is all we have. Go and sell what you have, and bring back what you can."

This boy actually is a concessionaire who has set up this little stand to sell his barley loaves and fish (similar to a lemonade stand). I believe that if the Lord really wanted to have the maximum amount, He would have taken the two hundred denarii and bought much more than five barley loaves and two fish. But the Lord intentionally takes the little boy's concession of five barley loaves and two fish. Look at what Jesus does: He prays over it. The text says He gives thanks. Watch this! Andrew thought that he could just give the loaves and the fish to Jesus and somehow He would have some control. But it would still not be enough. It is only a small portion.

Attitude Concerning Our Sense of Power

The reason that God cannot work miracles in the lives of most of His children is because we want to be in control. We want a life that we can manage. In other words, the only time we want God to take full control is when a sickness comes that the doctor cannot cure. Then, we want to say, "Father, I stretch out my hand so that everyone knows." When there are loved ones who spurn our love, who have turned their backs on our plans for them, then we call God and say, "Come, Lord, quickly and take care of this."

If we were to be honest, most of us would admit that we really want to control our own lives, and we only want God to show up in case of an emergency. Therefore, God does not do anything new and different, cathartic, cataclysmic, or life-changing because we are not going to give God that much control. Most of us Christians would not bother God—and don't want God to bother us—if He would just keep food on our tables, gas in our cars, our lights turned on, our health reasonably well, and our homes from being lost.

This is a sense of power and being in control. How many of us would say that we do not like the feeling of being in control?

Let me give you an example. My wife thinks that she can drive better than I can. She really does. So, whenever Van drives and I'm in the passenger seat, I am nervous! When Van drives, this is the only time I think about taking a tranquilizer. I believe that if I am at the wheel, I am in control. Likewise, when I'm driving, Van sits on the passenger side constantly pressing her feet to the floor as if there were brakes on her side. Van believes that when she is driving, she is in control.

Most of us are not in a great big hurry to give God control of every area of our lives. We say, "Lord, take control. Bless all the things I do not control." When things are going well, we want to give God some praise and keep on going. But this story is designed to show us that the prayer of thanksgiving that Jesus prayed is not designed just to feed the five thousand—because the next day, the crowd showed up again and Jesus said to them, "The only reason you showed up was to get something to eat."

What is the central point of the story? This little boy was sent out by his mom or his parents with a little bit of food to try to sell it as a concession to get something to live on. It is not the same idea as the

Old Testament story of a woman who made the last bit of meal and said, "We are going to die" (1 Kings 17:12). But it is the idea that God wants us to bring to Him the little that we have.

When Jesus gave thanks, He prayed—and they fed everyone. Notice again the contrast. Two hundred denarii would have given them just a little, remember? But the boy's concession is enough to give everyone enough until they are full, and then they take up twelve baskets of leftovers. What I am suggesting to you is that Jesus said to that boy, "You brought Me five loaves and two fish. Take these twelve baskets now, and sell them, and take care of yourself and your family."

Attitude Concerning Other People

First, the Lord is saying, "I do not want you to become hung up on what you already have." Secondly, He is saying, "I do not want you to work so hard just to get a sense of control or mastery on your situation. I want you to be concerned about blessing other people."

This whole story is about this unseen parent who sends this boy with a little and Jesus cares enough—just not about the five thousand. He meets their need, but the five thousand are not the real key here. The real key is that Jesus wants to honor the faith of this parent who sent the boy out with a little and Jesus sent the boy back with much. The song, "Ordinary People," says that little becomes much when it is placed in the Master's hand.

I want us to look at prayer as a sense of powerlessness in the presence of a powerful God. I want us to learn to go to Him as if we have nothing to offer but want to receive everything He has for us. I want us to see prayer as this: we are not in control. If you do not have cancer, you are still not in control of your health. If you get cancer, your health is not out of control because it is in the Master's hands. Every situation—relational, financial, spiritual, and physical—is in the Master's hands, because we are not in control.

Finally, it is all about concentrating on being a blessing to someone else. What an impact it would make in our lives if we woke up tomorrow and said, "You know, I want God to send me at least one person in whose life I can make a difference today. It may not be giving them five dollars. It may be giving them a call. It may be knocking on their door. It may be helping senior citizens with their groceries. But I

am going to start every day seeking to try to help at least one person."
And I can already tell you that you are going to receive a lot more than
you ever gave.

Questions to Consider

1. *Do you trust God to provide your needs?*

2. *Do you pray about your daily needs?*

3. *How do you respond when needs are not met immediately?*

10

Keys to Answered Prayer–Part 4

Philippians 2:2, 5; 4:2, 8

For our last lesson on "Keys to Answered Prayer," I want us to understand first that answered prayer begins in the mind. Second, our attitude in prayer is important. Third, anxiety or worry prevents our prayers. Finally, how we do apply what we've learned?

Philippians 2:1–5 says:

> If there be therefore any consolation in Christ, if any comfort of love, if any fellowship of the Spirit, if any bowels and mercies,
>
> Fulfill ye my joy that ye be [there it is] like-minded, having the same love, being of one accord, [and here it is again] of one mind.
>
> Let nothing be done through strife or vainglory; but in lowliness [there it is again] of mind let each esteem other better than themselves.
>
> Look not every man on his own things, but every man also on the things of others.
>
> Let this [what?] mind be in you, which was also in Christ Jesus. (KJV)

Answered Prayer Begins in the Mind

It is clear that when we are talking about God answering our prayers, answered prayer begins in the mind. If we really expect God to answer our requests, then how we think about those requests and how we present those requests will determine whether or not those requests are answered. Answered prayer starts in the mind. Joyce Meyer highlights the importance of the mind. "The mind is the leader or forerunner of all actions (see Romans 8:5). Our actions are a direct result of out thoughts. If we have a negative mind, we will have a negative life. If on the other hand, we renew our minds according to God's word, we will, as Romans 12:2 promises, prove out in our experience "the good and perfect will of God" for our lives."[6]

1. *The mind—your mind—is a place of defeat or victory (Prov. 23:7).* The way that you think determines whether you are victorious or whether you are defeated. This puts the responsibility of answered prayer on whom? On you! It is up to you whether or not your prayers are answered, and it begins in your mind. Therefore, you and I must be sure we believe that God can answer our prayers before we ask Him.

Several times in Scripture we see that the first century church prayed about things, yet did not believe that God would answer their prayers.

You may recall that when Peter was in prison, the church met at Mary's house and prayed fervently that God would release Peter. Suddenly there was a knock at the door, and Rhoda, the servant, answered and saw Peter at the door. And, Rhoda, full of joy, ran back and hollered, "Peter is at the door!" The Bible says that they responded with, "No, it cannot be him. He is in prison." She said, "No, I'm telling you, our prayers have been answered. Peter is at the door." And they said, "No, it's probably his spirit. Maybe he died and his spirit has come back" (Acts 12:12-16). Even in the first century church, they prayed without believing that God could answer their prayers.

Proverbs 23:7 says, "For as he [a man or a woman] thinketh in his heart, so is he." We need to understand that we literally become what we think—not all at once, not overnight, but over time. We become a product of our thought processes. A negative-thinking Christian will never be a victorious Christian. Likewise, the victorious-thinking Christian will never be a negative or a defeated Christian. Over time, we become whatever we think.

Our minds become the most important part of our prayer-answering process. We wonder if God answers prayer. Previously, I told you about the person who was praying for our friend with pancreatic cancer. He prayed, "Oh, God, heal him. Heal him, God. I know you can heal him, God. In Jesus' name, we cast out that pancreatic cancer."

Then, when he finished praying, he said, "You know, 90 percent of those who get pancreatic cancer die." Life and death is in the tongue. We say one thing with our mouths, but in our minds we don't believe what we are saying. Answered prayer begins in the mind.

2. *Oneness of mind is individual and congregational.* There are some things that God will never do in your family, your church, or your community unless there is oneness of mind. Oneness of mind is individual and congregational. When the day of Pentecost came in Acts, chapter 2, remember that the Bible says, they were all in one place, in one accord (Acts 2:1) [and of one mind]. It is possible for us, by the power of the Holy Spirit, to come together and think just like God thinks.

Unfortunately, we cannot agree. We have this idea that the church cannot be of one accord because all of us are individuals with different beliefs, different backgrounds, different ages, different educational values, and different economic strata. Therefore, how can we be so different and yet be of one accord? Well, guess what? The Holy Ghost, the power of God, can put the church in one accord.

We act as if it is impossible to think alike and to come together. It is not. God says that we have to have the same mind. That is the only way we can get individual and congregational prayers answered. We have to touch and agree on the same thing.

Attitude in Prayer is Important

Philippians 2:3 says, "Let nothing be done through strife or vainglory [selfishness]; but in lowliness [or humility] of mind let each esteem others better than themselves" (KJV).

The idea here is that even though someone may be a new member, we lift them high. Someone may not be our wealthiest member, but we lift them high because the strong bears the infirmity of the weak (Romans 15:1). Those who have the greater glory should give glory to those who have the lesser glory. It is topsy-turvy. It is upside down. In the world, we lift up the mighty, the powerful, and the strong. But in the church, it is the weak, the lowly, and the meek to whom we give glory.

Someone becomes our most important member because he/she may be the neediest one. And someone who has been around a long time becomes the weaker member because he/she has a lesser need then anyone else. That is what "humility of mind" means: you hold someone else in higher esteem than you hold yourself.

You do not have to be the big shot all the time. Sometimes, you can be the low one. The world is not going to go along with that, but the church ought not to be like the world.

In the South (which we call the "country"), there is a saying, "Lord, let there be no big I's and little you's." In other words, "Let everybody be of one accord." This is how prayers get answered. We should try to out-love the other person. We should try to get lower—not a false humility, but a genuine humility. We should try to get lower and lift someone else up higher.

1. *According to Philippians 2:3–4, we should be "other-centered."* We should esteem others higher than ourselves. Why is that so difficult for us? Why is it so hard for us to not take the low road? You may have heard the Irish song that says something like, "You take the high road and I'll take the low road and I'll be in Ireland before you." We never sing that song in church because all of us, in our own way, are looking for the high road. That attitude is the opposite of what God is calling for. He says that we ought to be other-centered.

"How are *you* doing?" Instead of wanting someone to always ask how *you* are doing, you should ask them how *they* are doing. Instead of asking, "What can the church do for me, what can the tribe do for me, what can the deacons do for me, and what can the Pastor do for me?" why not ask, "What can I do? What can I do to make the church better?"

Most of us are experts in tearing down, but we are not experts in building up. "What can I do?" Oftentimes, one of the trustees of the church just watches us walk right by a piece of paper lying on the floor, and not one of us picks it up. Members seem to have the impression that there is somebody around here who is paid to pick litter up. So they think, "I'm not going to stoop down with my pure hands and pick up dirty paper! I'm not going to go get bathroom tissue and put it in the ladies' restroom. Somebody gets paid to do that. I'm not going to soil my pretty fingers getting that tissue." The attitude we have is that "someone else can do it, not me. I want to be served."

The Bible says that Jesus came to serve. He did not come to lord over us but to humble himself. How many of us have that attitude? We may say, "You passed right by me and you did not open your mouth!" Well, you both have a mouth! The idea seems to be that the other person is obligated to speak first.

2. *Christ-centered.* Philippians 2:5 says, "Let this mind be in you, which was also in Christ Jesus" (KJV). Just imagine! Jesus gave up the wealth of heaven and became earth's slave! He had everything. Angels bowed down all the time worshipping Him. He created all things. In his letter to the Colossians, Paul wrote, "He is the image of the invisible God, the firstborn over all creation. For by Him all things were created that are in heaven or on the earth, visible and invisible, whether thrones or dominions or principalities or powers. All things were created through Him and for Him" (NKJV).

One day, Jesus took a towel, wrapped it around Himself, got a pail of water, and began to wash the disciples' feet. Peter said, "Lord, no! You will not wash my feet. You are above that." Jesus said, "If I do not wash your feet, you will have no part in this ministry." Then Peter got it and said, "Oh, Lord, wash not only my feet, but wash me all over (John 13:5–9)!"

All of us need to become primitive foot-washing Baptists who will say, "I can bow down and wash your feet." That is humility. This is talking about how prayers get answered. We have to be Christ-centered and other-centered.

3. *Obedience-centered.* Philippians 2:12 says that we ought to be obedience-centered:

Therefore, my beloved, as you have always obeyed, not as in my presence only, but now much more in my absence, work out your own salvation with fear and trembling. (NKJV)

I know some of this is not going to make sense, but to be a Christian is to live life in awe and wonder.

Every now and then, you ought to sit yourself in the presence of angels. Every now and then, you ought to get heavenly goose bumps because you are accessing contact from another dimension. This is not an everyday sameness. There is something mysterious, awe-filled, and wondrous about this life in Christ. Every now and then, you ought to be caught up in the mystery of it all. You cannot understand it, you cannot explain it, but you know it is a God thing. It is obedience. It is our attitude.

Anxiety Prevents Our Answers

Philippians 4:4 (NKJV) says, "Rejoice in the Lord always. Again I will say, rejoice!" The Christian ought to be a rejoicing person. People should look at a Christian and say, "You are always rejoicing. Every time I see you, you are rejoicing. I know you are going through difficulties, but you are always rejoicing. I know you do not have everything that everyone else has, but you always seem to be rejoicing. I know your health is not the best, but you are always rejoicing."

Most of us are not known for our rejoicing. We are known for our complaining. Nothing is ever quite right. "The ushers did not speak to me this morning." "Nobody handed me a bulletin." "It is too cold." "It is too hot." "It is too crowded." "Where is everybody?" "The choir is not singing well today." "Where is the deacon?" One would think that we do not have a God; we do not have a Christ; we do not have a heaven; we do not have the Holy Ghost; we do not have comfort; and we do not have experience. You would think that we are in this all alone, when in fact, a whole crowd of witnesses get up every day to tell you that you can make it. But we worry about what we do not have, what we cannot see, or what we do not know. What you ought to do is rejoice.

Rejoicing is a choice. I often hear that you have to look at a glass as half-full, not half-empty. That is an attitude. That is a way of thinking. Most of us have more than we ever had. We know more than we have ever known. We are blessed now more than ever. Then why can't we just rejoice in what God has already done? Paul said, "Rejoice always."

Philippians 4:5 says, "Let your moderation [or self control] be known unto all men" (KJV). Are you known as a Christian who is always under control? Or are you known more as a Christian who is always out of order? Good question!

1. *Worry is forbidden.* As a Christian, worry is never an acceptable response to any situation—no matter who does it or when. Do you know why? Because God is sovereign. We must never forget that God is sovereign. There is nothing that can happen to you and me that God has not already looked over and said, "All right, you and I together

can handle this." You are not alone. You are not on your own strength. Zechariah 4:6 is a good passage that says, "'Not by might nor by power, but by My Spirit,' says the Lord" (NKJV). God never asks you and me to do anything in our own strength but rather in God's power. Ephesians 6:10 says, "Be strong in the Lord and in the power of His might" (NKJV). It is not our strength but His strength.

2. *Prayer is encouraged.* Pray about everything. Just pray about it. Take your burdens to the Lord and leave them there. If you pray and do not doubt, He will surely bring you out. Take your burdens to the Lord and leave them there. God encourages prayer.

3. *Thanksgiving is required.* Pray with thanksgiving. That is required. In other words, our prayers are not finished until we thank God for the answer while we are still on our knees. "I want to thank You that You hear me." That is what Jesus said in John 17: "I want to thank You, Father, that You always hear Me. You always answer My prayer. Thank You for what You are going to do. Lord, I give You permission to work it out in Your own way. It is not how I want it done, but it is how You want it done, and I want to thank You. As a matter of fact, I want to thank You just for the blessing of sharing this burden with You. I have a God that I can go to any time and tell Him anything."

Another question for discussion is, "Why don't we take advantage of this precious privilege of prayer?" Many of us are more comfortable asking someone else to pray for us then we are praying for ourselves. We need each other's prayers. But no one else can tell God what you need like you alone can. You know some things, but some things you don't know. So you have to tell God what you need Him to know from your own lips. Someone else might twist what you are trying to express. "Well, Lord, bless him. But not all at once." "Teach him something, God." Someone else may put in something extra that you may not mean. But when you talk to God about yourself, you know how to talk to Him for yourself. "Pray for me. Pray for me." Sometimes we will not pray for anybody else, nor will we pray for ourselves.

4. *Telling Him everything is recommended.* "God, you know I have this problem with lust. I may not be able to tell anybody else about it, but God, I want You to know that I need Your help with this lust problem."

"God, I am stingy, and people think I am generous. You know I do not give nearly as much as I could. God, thank You for hearing my prayer about my stinginess."

"God, I am really selfish. People think I am a nice guy, but You know that I am selfish. I have to tell You that."

"Lord, I have to tell You that I am a gossip. I may seem like I am concerned about somebody, but God, You and I know that deep down in my heart, I love to discuss other folk's business. God, I want to tell You that in my heart, I am a gossip."

"God, I have to tell You something else. You know I am a peace-breaker. I just cannot stand when things are going well. If things are going well, I have to find something to tear it apart, because, Lord, I realize that I am a peace-breaker. I am always stirring up something."

How many of us are frank with God in prayer? How many of us pray to God like we do to other people? We never tell anybody who we really are and what we are dealing with. How many of us are like that with God? How many of us can only tell God the good stuff about ourselves—as if He does not know?

Imagine that you are a Christian, and every now and then you decide to do recreational drugs. You are not an addict anymore, but now and then you smoke a joint or take a drink. Or, every now and then you smoke a pack of cigarettes when you are on vacation. You don't smoke them anywhere else, but when you go on vacation, you take a pack with you. Do you tell God about it?

"Lord, I am a recreational drug user. Lord, I am a closet smoker. Lord, when I go to hotels, I turn on the porn station. I don't do it at home because my wife [or my husband] might see me. But on that business trip, I cannot wait to get in that room and turn it on."

Do you ever tell God that? "Well," we say, "God knows." No, no, no! Do you ever *tell* God? We know God knows, but do *you* know God knows?

Sometimes our anxiety and our desire to try to be cute in front of God keeps our prayers from being answered. We have got to be gut-level honest with at least one person in the universe. It would be nice to be honest with two. You and God. But if you cannot be honest with yourself, at least be honest with God.

5. *God guarantees peace.* If you tell God about it, do not hold anything back—just lay it out there. God says that when you get through with all of that, you will have peace.

How many of you have ever dealt with something very serious? You took it to God, and when you really knew that you had laid it at the feet of God, you had that peace that passes all understanding (Philippians 4:7). You honestly knew then that you had given it up to God, because from that moment on you did not worry about it anymore.

Applications

1. *Our minds must undergo major renovations.* Romans 12:2 says, "Be transformed by the renewing of your mind" (NKJV). Honestly, all of us, and I can say this without fear of contradiction, no matter where you are in your walk with God, you and I still need major renovation of our minds. We allow too much junk from the Internet, the television, the radio, and other sources to cloud our minds. Some of us watch television or listen to talk radio 24/7. That junk is in our minds, and we don't even realize it. If we watch any television, read any newspaper, or log onto the Internet, our minds are being messed up. We need major renovation because what we think is what we become. "Garbage in—garbage out."

2. *"Grand Re-Opening—Under New Management" (Phil. 2:5).* A major renovation may take quite a bit longer than you might think. It is not going to be a two-week, two-month, or even a two-year affair. After this renovation, however long it takes, we need to have a "Grand Re-opening—Under New Management." The new Manager of our mind must be the Lord Jesus Christ. Philippians 2:5 says, "Let this mind be in you." This is our entitlement: the very mind of Christ. You can think thoughts just like Jesus. You can have the wisdom of God. Imagine the way that God would do it, and you could do it that very same way. You can have God's perspective on anything. It is yours. What would Jesus do? Any of us can ask the question and get the answer.

Proverbs 3:13-14 says, "The greatest possession that anyone can have is wisdom." It is more precious than silver and gold. With wisdom, you can make wise choices—not 75 percent of the time, not 80 percent of the time—but every time. Every time!

3. *Jesus must guard our minds for us.* Philippians 4:7 says the Lord Jesus will guard your mind.

When I was doing an intensive study some years ago, the study offered a beautiful word picture for verse 7. It said that if you ask the Lord Jesus to guard your heart and your mind, no emotion will get lodged there that God did not put there. No thought can stay there if it is not God's thought.

The word picture is the idea that Jesus becomes a guard for your heart and mind. It is not an angel, not Moses, but the Lord Himself. Whenever a negative thought or negative emotion comes to you, the Lord Himself, in full dress like a soldier, will say, "There is a guard on duty. Halt. Who or what goes there?" That thought or emotion has to declare who it is. If it is not safe for you, Jesus says, "You cannot enter in!"

The Lord Jesus stands guard over your heart and mind. What a tremendous Warrior to have control of your emotions in your life without any cost—free of charge.

Questions to Consider

1. *Do you spend time clearing your mind before prayer?*

2. *Do you thank God before, during, and after prayer?*

3. *Do you praise God for answered prayer?*

11

The Lord's Prayer

John 17

The prayer in John 17 reveals our Lord's heart. This prayer contains the subjects that are important to Him. This prayer should become our prayer "mission statement."

John 17:1–26 (KJV) reads:

> These words spake Jesus, and lifted up his eyes to heaven, and said, Father, the hour is come; glorify thy Son, that thy Son also may glorify thee:
>
> As thou hast given him power over all flesh, that he should give eternal life to as many as thou hast given him.
>
> And this is life eternal, that they might know thee the only true God, and Jesus Christ, whom thou hast sent.
>
> I have glorified thee on the earth: I have finished the work which thou gavest me to do.
>
> And now, O Father, glorify thou me with thine own self with the glory which I had with thee before the world was.
>
> I have manifested thy name unto the men which thou gavest me out of the world: thine they were, and thou gavest them me; and they have kept thy word.
>
> Now they have known that all things whatsoever thou hast given me are of thee.
>
> For I have given unto them the words which thou gavest me; and they have received them, and have known surely that I came out from thee, and they have believed that thou didst send me.
>
> I pray for them: I pray not for the world, but for them which thou hast given me; for they are thine.

And all mine are thine, and thine are mine; and I am glorified in them.

And now I am no more in the world, but these are in the world, and I come to thee. Holy Father, keep through thine own name those whom thou hast given me, that they may be one, as we are.

While I was with them in the world, I kept them in thy name: those that thou gavest me I have kept, and none of them is lost, but the son of perdition; that the scripture might be fulfilled.

And now come I to thee; and these things I speak in the world, that they might have my joy fulfilled in themselves.

I have given them thy word; and the world hath hated them, because they are not of the world, even as I am not of the world.

I pray not that thou shouldest take them out of the world, but that thou shouldest keep them from the evil.

They are not of the world, even as I am not of the world.

Sanctify them through thy truth: thy word is truth.

As thou hast sent me into the world, even so have I also sent them into the world.

And for their sakes I sanctify myself, that they also might be sanctified through the truth.

Neither pray I for these alone, but for them also which shall believe on me through their word.

That they all may be one; as thou, Father, art in me, and I in thee, that they also may be one in us: that the world may believe that thou hast sent me.

And the glory which thou gavest me I have given them; that they may be one, even as we are one:

I in them, and thou in me, that they may be made perfect in one; and that the world may know that thou hast sent me, and hast loved them, as thou hast loved me.

Father, I will that they also, whom thou hast given me, be with me where I am; that they may behold my glory, which thou hast given me: for thou lovedst me before the foundation of the world.

O righteous Father, the world hath not known thee: but I have known thee, and these have known that thou hast sent me.

And I have declared unto them thy name, and will declare it: that the love wherewith thou hast loved me may be in them, and I in them.

John 17 is the true Lord's Prayer. I thought it would be good for us, as the body of Christ, to know what the Lord prayed. What were His concerns? I think that if our concerns match the Lord's concerns, we will experience more answered prayer.

Is it possible that we are not experiencing fervent answered prayer because what we are asking for does not match what the Lord would have us ask for? Is it possible that our agenda in prayer does not match the Lord's agenda? Is it possible that we have to change our prayer focus so we can match His? I think that we need to look at what interested the Lord. John 17 is a prayer. It is twenty-six verses, and together they constitute a prayer.

What is it that God was praying for through Jesus? Beginning with the first sentence, the prayer reveals our Lord's heart. It contains the subjects that are important to Him. It should also become our prayer mission statement. We need a mission statement about prayer. It should not come out of our concerns, but the things that concern the Lord. The late British pastor Martyn Lloyd-Jones sets the context of our Lord's Prayer. "In order that we may understand that petition offered on behalf of His followers by our Lord on the eve of His death, let me remind you of the context. Our Lord is about to go to His death on the cross so He prays for these men whom He is leaving behind in the world and He gives various reasons for praying for them. He reminds the Father of who they are; then He comes to the particular petitions for them."[7]

Giving the Father Glory

The first subject that Jesus talks about is that we are to pray so that our lives give God glory. The word "glory" is the Greek word *doxa,* which means to give weight to something or someone. When we give God glory, we give weight to God. In other words, God becomes our highest priority. God becomes our focus point. When you give weight to something, you give attention to it.

There was a saying in the '60s: when somebody was intellectually bright, we would say that he or she was "heavy." They were weighted intellectually. Our prayers should be weighted down with giving God glory. We ought to want to live in a way that our lives become a reflection of the glory of God. That is what Jesus was trying to convey in Matthew 5:16 when He said, "Let your light so shine before men, that they may see your good works" (NKJV) and do what? "Glorify your Father which is in heaven" (NKJV)! Give weight to Him. The whole idea of the Christian life is to draw attention to God.

We are reflectors. But Christians today seem to be more concerned about drawing attention to themselves. "Look at how well I sing!" "Look at how well I preach!" "Look at how large my church is!" "Look at how large the choir is!" "Look at how talented I am!" We are drawing attention to ourselves, and that is why we do not have drawing power. Jesus said, "As Moses lifted up the serpent in the wilderness (John 3:14), so if the Son of Man is lifted up then I will draw all men unto Me" (John 12:32). But we cannot draw people to Christ if you and I become the focus. We have to lift Him up.

In looking at John 17, verses 1, 4, 5, 10, and 22, Jesus is saying, "Father, all I want is to give You glory." What would happen if every wife decided to try to make her husband look good? What would happen if every husband worked to make his wife look good? What would happen if all parents worked to make their children look good? What would happen if all children worked to make their parents look good? What if each one of us decided that our emphasis would be lifting up somebody else?

Philippians 2:3 says it like this, "Esteem others better than yourself." What would happen if all of us made the commitment in the right spirit to try to out-love one another? We can do great things for God if we do not care who gets the credit. We should only give God the glory, and hold others in higher esteem than we hold ourselves.

When Jesus prayed, the first subject that He prayed about was giving God glory. That is what you and I are called to do: to give Him glory; to lift Him up. There is a song that says, "Lift Him up by living as a Christian should." Jesus wants to give glory to God.

Work of Ministry

Next, we notice that Jesus is concerned about the work of the ministry. In my book, *Congregation Driven Ministry*, there is a chapter titled "Motivational Ministry" that emphasizes Jesus' concern. Jesus said, "I must work the work of Him that sent Me while it is day. When night comes, no man can work" (John 9:4). In other words, Jesus understood that He had three years to do the job. Notice that Jesus was never in a hurry. He took time to pray, relax, and go on retreats. Jesus was never in a hurry, yet He was focused on getting the maximum done in the shortest amount of time.

Every one of us has a limited time on earth. Maybe I should not have told you that. I will tell you something else: the longer you live, the less strength you will have to do what God has called you to do. As you get older, the mind will want to do it, but the body will not cooperate. Consequently, we really have a diminishing window of opportunity.

Another truth is that when we are young, we have a lot of strength but no sense. When we get older, we have a lot of sense but no strength. Somewhere in the middle, we have to get it together with some sense and some strength. What Jesus is saying is, "While I have some sense and some strength, I have to do all that I am going to do."

That is why it is silly or backwards for someone to say, "Well, you know, I'm not ready yet. I'm not ready to change and do right. When I get ready, then I'm going to come to church. But I'm not ready to get saved yet. I don't want to live like that. I'm not going to have any fun. I want to do my thing. Sow my wild oats. Do my due. When I finish doing my due—do what I do—then I'm going to serve God."

Here's the problem: once you make up your mind to serve God, it is going to take a long time to get to where you know what you are doing. The longer you take to get started, the less you are going to get done. The truth is this: if you wait until you are forty-five to get serious, then you will have to overcome forty-five years of carnality. It will take you ten years to know that you are saved, ten more years to be assured of your salvation, then ten more years to know what your gift is. By that time, you are in the convalescent home!

1. *Share the gift of eternal life.* Jesus said, "I am trying to do as much as I can while I can." And He said, "I want to share the gift of eternal life; I want to manifest Your name to the world; I want to keep Your word" (John 17:6). All three of those statements are really three in one. Jesus said, "Now listen, the most important gift that I can give anyone is eternal life" (Romans 6:23).

We, as parents, have to give an account before the seat of God. This also includes grandparents and great-grandparents. We must stand before God and account for the fact that we gave too much materially to our children, grandchildren, and great-grandchildren and too little spiritually. We have to give an account of that. We worked hard to get them a secular education, but we did not put much emphasis on their Christian education. We will have to give an account that we went over hill and dale to get them to their extracurricular activities, but we let them decide whether or not they wanted to come to church.

When you stand before God, I imagine He will say, "Now tell Me, what was that about?" He will say, "I have time. We have all eternity. I have nowhere to go, so pull up a seat and let us discuss it for about three hundred years. I want you to tell Me: what was that all about?"

What are we going to tell Him? Are we going to say, "Well, God, you know, I didn't have much, so I didn't want my children to live like I lived." And the Lord would say, "You spent all that time trying to give them what you did not have, and now what you have, you did not pass on."

2. *Manifest His name to the world.* 1 John 2:15 reads, "Love not the world, neither the things that are in the world. If any man love the world, the love of the Father is not in him" (KJV). John is saying that the world system—that part of society that does not accept God—and the church are diametrically opposed to each other. In other words, the world system and the church are at odds. They are never going to agree on anything because they are going in two different directions. The things that the world thinks we should be tolerant of, the Bible says we ought to condemn. The things that the world says we ought to condemn, basically we should be tolerant of. We, as followers of Christ, do not take our cues from the world.

I cannot stand to hear Christians say, "I want to be politically correct." A saint says, "Well, at my job I have to be politically correct." And in hell sinners will be lifting up their eyes, because we were politically correct but they were eternally lost.

3. *Keep His word.* Sharing the gift of eternal life is what I want to do. Jesus says to manifest His name to the world, and to keep His word.

Prayer

In John 17:9, Jesus prays specifically by saying, "I pray for them"—and what? "Not … for the world but for those whom You have given Me" (NKJV).

1. *For believers.* In 1 John 2:19, Jesus said, "They went out from us, but they were not of us; for if they had been of us, they would have continued with us." Many times, we are trying to keep goats in the sheep corral. We try to make them happy. But a goat and a sheep will never get along. The church is so busy trying to keep the goats happy that the sheep are malnourished. You see, a goat will get by on entertainment. You "pop and lock" in church, and the goats like that. But goats do not like the word or anything serious.

Jesus said, "I have kept the ones that You gave me." And, "Not one was lost" (John 17:12). Oftentimes I wish I could help some churches, because many of them really believe that you can be saved today and lost tomorrow, then saved the next day, then lost again. They believe that we are saved one month and lost another month. Let me tell you something: you will never do anything for God like that.

It is not that you and I are saved and we can do anything we want to do. But, when we are saved, our eternity is secure. He does not have to save you once and then save you again. "What if I get out of God's hands?" Well, Jesus just said, "None are lost." That means you cannot get out of God's hand. If you can get out of God's hand, you were not in God's hand to begin with.

"How is the creature going to be stronger then the Creator? "I know I was saved, but God lost me. I vacillated, and I am lost. If I died now I would go to hell, because I cannot confess my sins while I am lost." Well, you do not get saved because you confessed all your sins. You are saved because Jesus saved you!

You have to know that you are saved to work for God. An unsure Christian is a do-nothing Christian. Jesus says, "I am praying for you" (Romans 8:34). That statement alone should comfort you, to know that the Lord is praying for you. Even when you do not pray for yourself, Jesus is praying. Hebrews 7:25 says, "He lives to make intercession." Jesus loves to call your name to the Father.

Have you ever gone through something where you did not even feel like praying? Were you mad at God? You would say anything, go where you wanted to, and you would say to God, "I am going to spite You, God. I am not going to pray. I am really going to spite You. I am not going to read the Bible. I am really going to mess You up, God. I am not going to church for three Sundays."

And God is saying, "You know what? I am praying for you. I am praying for you. You are in bad shape right now, but don't worry about it. I've got you covered."

When you are most vulnerable, Satan says, "Ah, she is not praying. She is mad at God. She is not going to church. I think I will sneak right in and steal her salvation." The devil comes to steal it and our God says, "No, it is sealed" (Ephesians 1:13). The devil cannot break the seal. When you are at your lowest and most vulnerable, that is when Jesus says, "I am praying. I have you covered." That is what Jesus says He is doing, and that is what He is doing. "I am praying." When we are most unlikable and most unlovable, that is when we need to be prayed for and prayed over.

Jesus is praying for believers. You may ask, "Why isn't He praying for everyone?" The answer is that Jesus knows everybody. The Bible says that He knows what is in man. He does not need anyone to tell Him. When Jesus says, "I am not going to waste time praying for you," He is saying, "I am praying for believers, because I did not leave the business of kingdom work in the hands of sinners, but in the hands of saints. So, I am praying for the saints." If we can get it, the world will eventually get it.

Tony Evans wrote a book a few years ago, and the title of this book is very interesting. It is titled *The Kingdom*. The author asks the question, "Is America going to hell because of the church?" His thesis is that the *world* is in the shape that it is in because the *church* is in the shape that it is in. God never called for the world to get better. But

God says, "If My people ... " (2 Chron. 7:14). We are so busy trying to love the world, but the world needs you to love God. Jesus says, "I am praying for believers."

2. *Be kept.* Jesus is also praying that you and I would be kept. I am not talking about being kept since you were sixty-five or seventy years old.

I want you to put your mind on rewind—go back to when you were twenty- or thirty-something. Here is the deal. You knew the right things to do; but every now and then, you did not want to do right. You knew right from wrong; but every now and then, you would still want to be in the wrong.

Come on; put your mind on rewind. I'm talking about before you were strong. Jesus is saying, "I am praying that you be kept when you do not want to be" (John 17:12). I know you are not going to get rid of the Bible, I know you will not admit it. But there are some occasions when a saint does not want to be kept. "God cannot keep me, because I do not want to be kept." You are on the prowl. You are looking. You are trying to catch. You are out there. You are not talking about sanctification. You are talking about "wigglefication."

The Lord says, "Now, you know, she is going through something right now, so I am going to have to rearrange some things and do some navigating. I have to do some blocking." You are on the cell phone calling, trying to get a connection, and all of a sudden the Holy Ghost drops the call. I'm telling you: He is trying to keep you. You have already made plane reservations to go out of town, and you only have the weekend. When you get to the airport, the plane is delayed for an hour—then two hours, then three hours. You are then informed that you have to wait for another plane and that the airline is going to place you in a hotel overnight. You say, "I might as well go back home!" The Lord has blocked you. He is trying to keep you.

We have to be honest. We do not always do right because we want to do right. Sometimes the Lord has to do right for us.

3. *Joy.* The other subject that this prayer covers is joy. A joyless Christian is a contradiction in terms. What makes us attractive is this: the world watches us as we are going through our stuff. They know you are not getting along with some people. They know things are not going right. Yet your personality is pretty much always the same. They

cannot tell whether you have money or not, because you pretty much always have the same demeanor. They cannot tell if you and the "old lady" or "old man" are getting along or not, because you always act the same.

But the joyless Christian walks around somber:

"How was service yesterday, Brother?"

"It was all right."

"How are you doing today?"

"Man, do not bother me. Leave me alone."

The world will say, "Wow! Last week he was cheery and jolly. Now he's depressed. I guess God is not working for him now."

Christians are to be witnesses. This is what I mean when I say that a Christian should have an "in-spite-of" praise. You are not always going to be up. I don't have to tell you that. You are not always going to be well. I know you like prosperity teaching and preaching. I know you like it. It sounds good, but you are not always going to be well. You are not always going to have all the money you need. You are not always going to be the most popular person on the block. You have to have an in-spite-of praise. And no matter what is going on around you, you still should have your head up.

The only time you and I ought to start "tripping" is if Jesus gets depressed. Have you ever prayed and the Lord said, "Hey, man, you know, I'm not having a good day"? Suppose you called up heaven and the Holy Ghost said, "Hey, man, I'm not taking calls from anybody right now. Call back later." Suppose you start getting the Son, the Holy Ghost, and the Father all saying, "This thing is out of My hands." If you get that from the Father, the Son, and the Holy Ghost, then it is time to trip. "Jesus is on medication, man." But as long as heaven is all right and God is in control, don't you worry about it. I heard the Lord say, "I got this. It might be hard for you, but it is not heavy to Me. I can handle this."

4. *The word.* Jesus prayed that we might make time and space for the word. The greatest contribution you and I can make is to make time for God's word in our lives. However, don't worry about it if you haven't memorized a lot of Scripture and you can't find everything that everyone asks you to find. Don't let that bother you. "But I can't quote

like she can. I can't quote like he can. You said, 'Nehemiah,' and she can go right to it."

So what? It's not how much Scripture you know—it's how much Scripture you live out in your daily life. It's not how much you have in your head—it's how much you have in your heart. What I am trying to say is that if you do not know all the Bible verses now, don't be discouraged. If you learn one verse a week, in six years you will be a brand-new creature. Jesus says, "I want you to get the Word."

5. *Sanctification.* In John 17:17, Jesus is saying, "I want you to be sanctified." In 1 Thessalonians 4:3, Paul writes, "For this is the will of God, your sanctification: that you should abstain from sexual immorality" (NKJV). What Paul is saying here is, "Sanctify yourself, or set yourself apart for God."

6. *Latter-day saints.* In John 17:20, Jesus is praying for the "latter-day saints"—which are not the Mormons. The Mormons claim to be latter-day saints, but they are not—they are "latter-day ain'ts." Saints are those who put all their confidence in Jesus. The Mormons think as highly of Joseph Smith as they do Jesus.

Jesus said, "I pray for them. I do not pray for the world but for those whom you have given me, for they are yours. I do not pray for these but for all those who will believe in me through their word" (John 17:9,20 NKJV). Jesus is talking about us. We are the authentic latter-day saints, because we are the ones who came as the result of the ministry of others. We have to get these names right. The Mormons are *not* latter-day saints. We are! Jesus is saying, "I am praying for them who are going to believe on Your word." This is what "latter day" refers to—those coming afterwards.

7. *Unity.* Then Jesus said, "I pray for unity" (John 17:11). Jesus prayed that we all might be one. There will be no schism in the body: one accord, one mind, one spirit, one direction, one desire, one hope, one lord, one faith, and one baptism. We will all be one. There will not be some of us over here and some over there. There will be no cliques and no "big I's and little you's." One! That is the prayer. Oneness! We will be all together, like the Three Musketeers: "All for one and one for all." No one will be left behind.

8. *Join Him in heaven (see John 14:1–6).* Jesus also said, "My prayer is that they will join Me in heaven" (John 17:24). Everybody wants to

go to heaven, but nobody wants to die. Jesus prays that one day we will all join Him in heaven. Since we are all going to die, the Bible says it is important. Jesus wants us to come to heaven, but we are trying to stay down here for 113 years, on thirteen medications three times a day. We have a walker, an ambulance, a cot, and a gurney. And we are still saying, "I just want to be here one more year."

9. *Love one another.* Last, Jesus says that He wants us to love one another (John 17:26). It would be wonderful if you and I make a renewed commitment to love one another.

Prayer

Father, I pray right now that the prayer that Jesus prayed in John 17 will become our prayer.

In Jesus' name. Amen.

Questions to Consider

1. Are you praying in agreement with the Lord?

2. What is your prayer focus?

3. Does your prayer time lead you to share your faith with others?

12

A Model for Praying

Luke 22:39–45

The garden of Gethsemane. If John 17 is the Lord's Prayer, then the prayer that Jesus prayed in the garden of Gethsemane is a Model Prayer. It is a prayer for all of us to look at as an example when we are dealing with the things of life. I believe it will bless you.

> Coming out, He went to the Mount of Olives, as He was accustomed, and His disciples also followed Him. When He came to the place, He said to them, "Pray that you may not enter into temptation."
>
> And He was withdrawn from them about a stone's throw, and He knelt down and prayed, saying, "Father, if it is Your will, take this cup away from Me; nevertheless not My will, but Yours, be done." Then an angel appeared to Him from heaven, strengthening Him. And being in agony, He prayed more earnestly. Then His sweat became like great drops of blood falling down to the ground.
>
> When He rose up from prayer, and had come to His disciples, He found them sleeping from sorrow. Then He said to them, "Why do you sleep? Rise and pray, lest you enter into temptation." (Luke 22:39–46, NKJV)

I just happened to hear about the story of the United Airlines jet flying from Denver, Colorado, to Phoenix, Arizona. They experienced such great turbulence that the pilot had to abort the flight, turn around, and go back to Denver. It was so much turbulence that one of the crew members was injured, as was a female passenger. The crew member's injuries included blood running from her eye, her forehead, and her ear. She said that the turbulence was so rough that she really thought this would be their last flight.

I thought about that, because you and I have to face turbulence in life. When turbulence comes, we say to ourselves, "This is it. We are not going to make it." The Lord is teaching through this prayer that no matter how terrible the turbulence gets, if we follow some basic instructions in this passage, we can handle turbulent times.

Most of the time, our response when something occurs is that we really think that this is the worst thing that could have happened to anybody at any time. When something happens to us, we feel like this: "There is no one in the world who has ever had to deal with this situation as I have." Often we feel like we are being picked out to be picked on, and we begin to have pity parties. We begin to become introverted. We not only stop reaching out to others, we stop reaching out to God, because we feel like "nobody knows the trouble I've seen."

But one of the things this passage says to us is that no matter what you are going through, and no matter how devastating it is, none of us will ever go through what the Lord went through. I do not care how ravenous the cancer might be that invades your body, you will never go through what our Lord went through. I do not care how devastating that divorce was—even if you've lost everything—you will never go through what our Lord went through. Your employer may have raked you over the coals and messed you up, but you will never go through what our Lord went through. Your child might be climbing Fool's Hill, never to come down again, but whatever you are going through is nothing like what the Lord went through.

So, whenever anything devastating happens to us, it hits us like turbulence. The one thing we have to say to ourselves is, "If it's not fatal, then it's not final," and it can still be fruitful. In other words, that initial hit (let's face it, we're all human) might knock you down for a moment, and you might lose your bearings. But you ought to get back up and say, "Whatever this is, it is not anything like what the Lord went through."

As a matter of fact, Paul wrote, "For our light affliction is but for a moment, is working for us a far more exceeding and eternal weight of glory. (Second Corinthians 4:17, NKJV) Whatever it is! Paul is saying, "If you look at the suffering of the Lord, and then look at what you are going through, I have two words for you: 'light' and 'momentary.'" In other words, it is not as heavy as what the Lord went through, and it won't last nearly as long. Light and momentary! It might not feel like it to you, but from God's perspective, it is light and momentary.

Prepare to Enter God's Presence (Place/Posture)

As Jesus modeled in the garden of Gethsemane, you have to prepare to enter God's presence. That means entering an appropriate place and assuming an appropriate posture. Prayer requires a personal discipline that most of us are just not willing to adopt. Because prayer is not easy, most of us do not want to engage in it.

That first prayer that Mom or Dad taught us—"Now I lay me down to sleep, I pray the Lord my soul to keep. If I should die before I wake, I pray the Lord my soul to take"—is often the extent of how we teach our children to pray. That's it. But that does not really prepare them for the difficulties of life. That is a kindergarten or a pre-kindergarten prayer. That is not high school, college, or postgraduate prayer. That prayer will not get you through the dark days of life. It just will not do it.

So the first thing the model prayer shows us is that prayer ought to become such a discipline that you and I give ourselves to it as a custom. Verse 39 says, "As He was accustomed" (NKJV). In other words, it was His custom. He had a certain place and a certain posture that He used when He entered into prayer.

Notice that Jesus said, "I and the Father are one (John 10:30). When you see Me, you see the Father. The work that I do is not just Me doing it, but the Father does it through Me. I must work the works of Him that sent Me while it is day" (John 9:4). I mean, you get the impression that there is no space between Father and Son in Their relationship, right? Guess what? That did not just happen. That is discipline. The text says it was His custom to go to the Mount of Olives down by the Kedron Valley; it was His custom to go to that particular spot and enter into prayer.

I ask you again: Do you have a certain place that you designate as your prayer ground? A place that, when you get there, God knows that you and God mean business? I know you can say, "Well, I pray on Highways 280, 101, or 880." I am not talking about that kind of prayer. There is no way you can concentrate on talking to God and weave in and out of traffic. You have to set aside time, go to a place, and assume a posture. In Jesus' day, people did not pray just on their knees. They prayed with their face to the ground in total surrender. Just like a burnt offering, they were giving themselves to God. You cannot pray riding around, looking, and shopping at the sales rack. You can not see what is on clearance and what is not on sale as you talk to God. ("Lord, lead me to the rack that is lower-priced than this.")

There has to be a posture of surrender when you pray. Then there must be a place in which you pray where God knows you mean business. It says here in Luke 22:39 that Jesus went to the Mount of Olives, which was His custom. You have to give yourself to prayer, and then prayer becomes a discipline.

It is not surprising that many of us never grow to spiritual maturity because we just do not put enough time into prayer. We just do not give ourselves to spiritual things so that we can mature in them. It seems as if we want a "convenient Christianity."

When the Crystal Cathedral first started in Southern California, it was a drive-in ministry. Robert Schuller started the Crystal Cathedral in the parking lot of an old drive-in theater. As you drove in, he would give you a Scripture and a prayer. You would then leave your offering and drive off. And the Crystal Cathedral became an $18-million-a-year business. Robert Schuller began his ministry by making Christianity convenient. On your way to Venice Beach, you could stop by and get Psalm 23, a quick blessing, leave your tithes, and continue on.

But listen: a convenient Christianity is not a sufficient Christianity. God is not calling us to convenience. He is calling us to consecration. You cannot get consecrated just coming to God when it is convenient. How much time are you spending with Him? Are you spending so much time with the Lord that you are beginning to look like Him from the inside out?

At Pilgrim Baptist Church, one of our couples has been married for fifty-seven years. Sometimes, when the light hits them just so, they look alike. Sometimes folks say, "Is that your brother?" Or, "Is that your sister?" They have been married for so long that they have begun to look alike. Can I ask you this? Have you been spending so much time with the Lord that you are beginning to look like Him? Colossians

1:15 says that He wants us to be the express image of the Lord Jesus: "Christ in you, the hope of glory" (Col. 1:27, NKJV).

Notice, also, that the text says that you must prepare to enter into God's presence. Just as athletes warm up their muscles before they begin to run, the Christian must warm up to enter God's presence. It is amazing the number of us who say, "Well, you know, I pray while I am, you know, watching television or listening to my iPod." Or, "When I'm on the computer and the screen goes blank, I say a quick prayer. Then I get back to what I was doing." Come on! You cannot do that. You have to prepare to enter God's presence. It takes time for you to warm up. I mean, honestly, it takes ten minutes to get your thoughts right. Come on! Have you ever gotten down to pray and thought, "Well, I need to write that check; that bill is due; I have to check on something in the oven … " It takes ten minutes just to get your mind right. Then it takes another ten minutes to get it out of you. Another ten minutes to get onto it, and by then, you're nodding off. Come on! You wake up an hour later and realize you fell asleep. If you ever want to cure insomnia, all you have to do is take a Bible to bed with you, because as soon as you start reading, the devil will put you right to sleep.

Praise Him for Past Blessings, Present Help (Custom)

In the model prayer, we also have to praise Him. Praise Him for past blessings and present help. Praise has to be a vital part of prayer.

Let me give some examples of praise:

- When God has done something for you, you ought to have a "*rescue*" praise. Praise God for rescuing you.

- When God blesses you though you have not been that good, you ought to have an "*in-spite-of*" praise.

- When things are not going well and you cannot see God moving, you ought to have an "*anyhow*" praise.

Praise is a vital part of prayer. You must thank God for what He has already done in order to get ready for what God is bringing to you next.

For example, let's say you have a child who never says, "Thank you." After a while you say to yourself, "I am not giving this child anything." God is the same way. If you cannot say thank you for last night's lying down and this morning's rising, and you cannot praise God for a reasonable portion of health and strength, you have no business asking Him for anything. You must praise Him for what He has already done *before* you start asking Him for something else.

Put It All on the Line (Request Made Known)

In the garden, Jesus asked His disciples to wait while He prayed. Then He went about a stone's throw away from His disciples. Here is the visual that you might get out of this. There are some things that you have to pray about alone, because nobody can pray about them for you like you can. Notice this: one of the reasons the disciples fell asleep is because they could not enter into the seriousness of this prayer. There are some people whom you ask to pray for you, but they cannot understand the depth of your situation. Even if they did pray, it would be one of those quickie prayers because they really do not understand. There are some requests that even you cannot adequately articulate. You do not understand it yourself.

Sometimes, even though there are others who love you, there are some battles that you have to fight in prayer all by yourself. No one else can tell God what you are dealing with like you can. Not your spouse; not your children; not even your siblings. There are some things that you and God have to work out by yourselves in prayer.

Jesus said to His disciples, "You stay here." They couldn't go there anyway. You have got to learn to pray for you.

So Jesus went alone to pray. Now, listen to what He said: "Father, if there is any other way to affect human salvation other than going to that cross, let it be so. Father, if you can think of any other way to bring men and women back to You, other than Me going through the devastation of that old rugged cross, let it be so. Father, You being God, if You can come up with a Plan B, please do it" (Luke 22:42, paraphrased).

You see, most of us only look at Jesus as God. We do not look at Him as being a man. The authors of the Nicene Creed, AD 325, wrote that Jesus Christ, the Son of God, was fully man and fully God—with no mixture of the two. We must see in this passage not Jesus the Deity, but Jesus the man.

Listen, Jesus got tired. Remember at the well? He was tired. He was not faking it. He was tired. When He got hungry, He was not just acting hungry. He was hungry. When He wept, He was not just acting like He was crying. He wept. And when his disciples hurt Him, they really hurt Him. When He said, "Where is your faith?" He was hurt. He was a man. When He said to God, "If there is a Plan B, give it to Me," He was a man.

Jesus went to the cross. He died on Friday, stayed in the ground all day Saturday, and got up early Sunday morning. We don't even think about the devastation of the cross. It was the cruelest death that anybody could ever die. So, Jesus, being a man, prayed, "God, if there is any other way You could do it … do it."

We take our salvation so lightly. "I will go to church, *if* I please." "I will serve, *if* I please." "If I do not want to, I do not have to." "Nobody can tell me what to do." We do not understand that Jesus suffered for us: the just for the unjust, the sinless for the sin-filled. Jesus said, "This thing is so mighty that if there is any way around it, I want it." He was a man.

He prayed so hard that great drops of blood poured out of His skin like sweat (Luke 22:44). The writer of Hebrews took this up and said, "In your struggle against sin, you have not yet resisted to the point of shedding your blood" (Heb 12:4, NIV). In other words, the writer is saying that you are not trying to live life so earnestly that blood drips out of you like sweat. You are not trying that hard. But Jesus did. He prayed until He sweated blood.

When you put the gospels together, it appears that Jesus prayed three times. In Matthew 26:40, He came back to His disciples and said, "Could you not wait?" I mean, all Jesus needed was some human companionship. No, they couldn't enter into the devastation of what Jesus was dealing with. What Jesus was saying to them was, "I know you cannot feel it like I feel it, but at least you can watch with Me. You can be there for Me. You may not be able to carry any of My burden, but I need to look around and see that at least you are concerned enough to come and see about Me."

Jesus put it all on the line: "If it be possible, let this pass. Not My will but Yours be done" (Matt. 26:42).

Let me ask you this: have you ever known what God wanted you to do, but you honestly did not want to do it? Yet, you wrestled with it long enough to conclude that it was best for you to go ahead and do it.

You have not yet started living the Christian life until you run up against some things that you do not want to do. Don't pretend that every time God tells you to do something, your response is, "Here am I. Send me." Liar, liar, pants on fire! That is not the way it is! Sometimes God tells us to go somewhere we do not want to go. And there are some things that God tells us to give up. Come on, now—you don't want to give it up, and I don't either. There are some pet sayings that you and I, if we could, would hold onto. Do not act like you are trying to give everything up. Some of you are still holding onto something.

But Jesus put it all on the line. He said, "Listen, I do not want to do it. But if this is Your will, then I love You enough, I trust You enough, to do what You want more than what I want." Listen, saints: that is living the Christian life. It is not always agreeing with what God wants to do in your life. But it is wrestling with it and coming to this conclusion: "If the Lord says yes, I am going to say yes." The only place to come to this is in prayer.

In sharing, I admit that there were some times when God told me to do some things that I had to pray long and hard about. Not that I did not think they were the right things to do, but I knew they were not going to be easy things to do.

Sometimes the Christian life is difficult because people really do not want to do what God tells them to do. So you have to wrestle with yourself. Remember Jacob? He wrestled with the angel and told him, "I am not going to turn you loose until you bless me" (Genesis 32:26). And sometimes, saints, there will be some things you are going to have to deal with in which the only victory will be wrestling with God about it all night long. Then, by the time the morning light comes, you will say, "Not my will, but Yours, be done."

Sometimes you just have to fast and pray about something because you really do not want to go there. But you know if you do not go there with God, the alternative is not going to be pleasant. So you wrestle with it and you cry over it. But you do not give it up until God blesses you. That is what He is trying to say to us: put it all on the line.

Parental Sovereignty (Your Will, Not Mine)

Then, there is a parental sovereignty. "Not my will, but Yours, be done." This has nothing to do with the lesson, but I want to challenge you with this: I believe that, if you are a child of God, there is so much that God wants to do in you, through you, and for you. I believe that. I believe what Jesus said:, "I came that you might have life, and have it more abundantly" (John 10:10, paraphrased). I believe that the average saints are living well beneath their privilege.

I want to challenge you to think about this: how much more could you do in life? I am not talking about only in the spiritual realm, but also, for example, how much more education could you have (even at your age)? What greater risks could you take in life to expose yourself to things that you have never dealt with? How many of us are living lives of mediocrity when excellence lies before us?

If we are not careful, saints, we will get into such a routine that all we are willing to do is go to work, come home, watch television, do some community work, come to church a couple nights a week, enjoy Saturday, come to church on Sunday, and then repeat this routine until the weeks become months and the months become years and the next thing you know, you are retiring, getting sick, and dying.

There is more to life than a gold watch at the end of forty years of service. It has absolutely nothing to do with how much money you make or where you live. I am talking about coming to a point where you become all that you can be.

I think we have become too satisfied with "average" and "mediocre." God has said, "I have abundant life for you" (John 10:10). We have gotten so accustomed to just going through the motions—routine, routine, routine. You are about to routine yourself to death. I am telling you that you are in a rut. In other words, you are stuck!

All you are doing is like that rat in a maze—just going through the motions. God is telling you, "I might allow some turbulence to come into your life to shake you up. Because any other way, you are not going to do it."

Some of you eat the same thing on Monday; the same thing on Tuesday; the same thing on Wednesday; the same thing on Thursday; and the same thing on Friday. On Saturday, you invite the family; on Sunday, you decide to go out. That is all of January. Then February. Then March. Routine.

Just as routine happens in our everyday lives, the same thing is happening in our spiritual lives. We read a few verses, say a prayer, go to church, and go to Bible study. All I am saying is that God wants more.

Is there anyone who is just tired of the routine? Is there anyone who can just honestly confess, "Pastor, I am stuck." Is there anyone who would not mind saying, "I am in a rut. I am just going through the motions." I believe this text is teaching that we are to wrestle with God through prayer until we get His direction for our life situation.

And then, Jesus gets up. Here is the good news of the story. He was man. So He had to put on His clothes as a man. He had to go through this humiliation. They laughed at Him. They said in Matthew 27:42, "If you are God, why not come down off that cross?" He had to go through that humiliation, that taunting. They spat on Him, pulled His beard out, and stabbed Him. But Jesus stayed there, because His preparation in the garden got Him ready for the cross.

Press On ("Whatever")

The turbulence that you have been going through and the hell that you have been catching is divinely designed to get you to the point where no matter what comes your way, you can say, "Whatever! I am pressing on!"

That is what prayer is designed to do. That is what God is trying to get you and me to understand. "Oh, God. I hope that does not happen! If I lose my job, I will just die. I will have no benefits!" But if the job shuts down tomorrow—"whatever."

"I love my children and I want them to do well, but if they decide to go against my teaching, I am going to press on—whatever."

"I love my spouse, and I know she loves the Lord. But if she decides not to serve God, I am pressing on—whatever."

If sickness comes: "whatever."

Financial setback: "whatever."

And that is when you say, "Come on, let's go. Let's get up and let's go. The enemy is coming, but he has no part in me, because I am getting ready to go and do what I can do." That is what Jesus models for us.

No matter what comes, make a point of finding a designated place where you and God can meet. It does not matter if it is your kitchen, your bedroom, or your closet. Designate a place where you and God can meet. Learn to wrestle with Him to the point that He gets you out of that lethargic, routine, mundane, mediocre life. Ask God to do something in you so that you won't just be killed by routine.

"Lord, burn a bush somewhere that I can see."

"Lord, give me a Damascus-road experience."

"Lord, come by where I live and tell me to follow You." ("And He will enable you to become fishers of men.")

"Lord, do something different. I am tired of mediocrity."

If you give God permission to do that, and then you are willing to wrestle with Him over and over and over, and on and on and on, you will get to the place where, no matter what the devil or any of his imps or his minions or someone who is working for him does, you can say, "Sheesh—whatever."

God bless you.

Questions to Consider

1. *Have you read Luke 22:39–45?*

2. *Do you identify with Jesus or the disciples?*

3. *Does your time in prayer enable you to face difficulties better?*

Conclusion

The motivation for prayer must be in response to the love of God.

The goodness of God should lead us to want to talk with Him.

The grace of God should beckon us into His presence.

Jesus told His first disciples that He would no longer refer to them as servants, but as His friends (John 15:15). Friends desire to spend quality time with each other. What a friend we have in Jesus!

His coming was to save us.

His death is to redeem us.

Prayer keeps us in contact with Him — who loves us with cords that will not let us go.

The saints in all ages have witnessed the power of prayer to change themselves and others.

Prayer is the key, and prayer unlocks the door to the purposeful, powerful life of faith.

When we learn to pray, the answer is found.

As children, we were taught to say grace as soon as we could join a few words together. Later, we would not climb into bed without closing the day by talking to God. But when we come of age, the call to prayer is absent in the home and most everywhere else.

When we had prayer in school, there was an absence of guns. Now there is an absence of prayer and the presence of guns!

I offer prayer, again, for those of us who desire a revival in our lives, churches, nation, and world.

If prayer becomes more common in just a few believers, then the effort spent in bringing about this work will not be in vain.

Let us pray!

Notes

Chapter 1
Wilkerson, Bruce. *The Prayer of Jabez,* Page 11.

Chapter 3
Omartian, Stormie. *The Prayer That Changes Everything*, Page 9.

Chapter 5
Spurgeon, Charles. *The Power in Prayer*, Pages 76–77.

Chapter 8
Lee, Kerwin B. *Winning the Battle Over Negative Emotions*, Page 124.

Chapter 9
Jakes, T.D. *Reposition Yourself, Living Life Without Limits*, Pages 88–89.

Chapter 10
Meyer, Joyce. *Battlefield of the Mind*, Page 118.

Chapter 11
Lloyd-Jones, Martyn. *Sanctified Through the Truth*, Page 7.

Bibliography

Hunt, T.W. *The Doctrine of Prayer*. Nashville, Tennessee: Convention Press, 1986.

Jakes, T.D. *Reposition Yourself Living Life Without Limits*. Atria Books, New York: Atria Books, 2007.

Lloyd-Jones, Martyn. *Sanctified Through the Truth: The Assurance of Our Salvation*. Westchester, Illinois: Crossway Books, 1989..

Lee. Dr. Kerwin B. *Winning the Battle Over Negative Emotions*. Lithonia, Georgia: Orman Press, 2003.

Meyer, Joyce. *Battlefield of the Mind*. New York: Faith Words, 1995.

Omartian, Stormie. *The Prayer That Changes Everything: The Hidden Power of Praising God*. Eugene, Oregon: Harvest House Publishers, 2004.

Spurgeon, Charles. *The Power in Prayer*. New Kensington, Pennsylvania: Whitaker House, 1996.

Spurgeon, Charles. *Praying Successfully*. New Kensington, Pennsylvania: Whitaker House, 1997.

Wilkinson, Bruce. *The Prayer of Jabez: Breaking Through to the Blessed Life*. Sisters, Oregon: Multnomah